BLITZED

by Blessings

To Travis
Blessings!
Read last Chapter!

"*Bill Glass has been a hero of mine for over fifty years. As I have read Blitzed By Blessings that level of hero worship has been elevated dramatically. What a book! What a life! What a man!*"

Pat Williams

Senior Vice President, Orlando Magic

Author, *Bear Bryant on Leadership*

Bill Glass
3 John 2

BLITZED
by *Blessings*

A Journey to Strengthening
Your Inner Core

BILL GLASS

Advantage®

Published by Advantage, Charleston, South Carolina.
Member of Advantage Media Group.

ADVANTAGE is a registered trademark and the Advantage colophon is a trademark of Advantage Media Group, Inc.

Printed in the United States of America.

ISBN: 978-1-59932-242-1
LCCN: 2010916685

This publication is designed to provide accurate and authoritative information in regard to the subject matter covered. It is sold with the understanding that the publisher is not engaged in rendering legal, accounting, or other professional services. If legal advice or other expert assistance is required, the services of a competent professional person should be sought.

Advantage Media Group is proud to be a part of the Tree Neutral™ program. Tree Neutral offsets the number of trees consumed in the production and printing of this book by taking proactive steps such as planting trees in direct proportion to the number of trees used to print books. To learn more about Tree Neutral, please visit www.treeneutral.com. To learn more about Advantage's commitment to being a responsible steward of the environment, please visit www.advantagefamily.com/green

Advantage Media Group is a leading publisher of business, motivation, and self-help authors. Do you have a manuscript or book idea that you would like to have considered for publication? Please visit www.amgbook.com or call 1.866.775.1696

DEDICATION

I am dedicating this book to Pete Redmon. We married beautiful sisters and think of each other as brothers. Without his encouragement, I would have never even attempted this book.

ACKNOWLEDGEMENTS

To my wonderful granddaughter, Katy McEachern. She typed this manuscript more than 10 different times, making edits, version changes, and valuable suggestions. Katy told me, "It was hard for me to type at times, since I was trying to see the computer through tears."

Denis Boyles, Editorial Director at Advantage Media Group, was gracious enough to personally, masterfully edit this book. Denis typically oversees projects while other editors make the changes, but he was intrigued enough to edit this one himself.

Special thanks to Michelle Pyle, who was the Managing Editor who did a great job of sheparding the whole project.

TABLE OF CONTENTS

INTRODUCTION

This autobiography is basically a recounting of the blessings of God over a 75 year life. Many things that happened early are only capped off by telling "the rest of the story." I've had to leave out many important people and factors, which should be included in a book of blessings, but there is not room to include all or even most of God's work witnessed by me in my 75 years. It has left me rejoicing because I have been blitzed by blessings.

From the beginning, my life has been an "all-out blitz." Always in a hurry, always trying to get the most done, always seeking to make the greatest difference, and always squeezing the most out of life. Always blitzing for the Lord, I wasn't satisfied to work in one prison but would try to handle three, six, 10, or 20 at a time.

Let me explain: The purpose of the blitz is to bring the ultimate pressure on the quarterback, with additional pass rushers crashing into the quarterback before he has time to pick out an open receiver.

Normally, there are four pass rushers—the defensive tackles and ends firing at top speed through, over or around the blockers and rushing or sacking the quarterback. We're trained to "lay our ears back" on any obvious passing down, like third and long, the first one to the quarterback wins! Any quarterback in the NFL will complete the pass, given enough time to find the open man. But on passing downs we will add a linebacker to the rush, calling him a blitzer. We may add one, two or three linebackers, and on rare occasions even defensive backs. This is called an all-out blitz. That's where I've lived most of my life.

TURN A BLIND EYE TO FAILURE

In February of 2010 I experienced a close brush with death. My colon had become obstructed and they had to remove nine feet of it, which was most of my colon. The doctor told me it was a miracle I didn't die. Recuperation was long and difficult, but it gave me my first chance ever to think, pray, and even keep a journal. One line from it reads: "For the last three weeks I've felt like a beached whale, only able to open one eye slowly."

You'll never know how difficult that is for someone who has been living life as an all-out blitz. Wide open and full speed ahead—that had been my life—a whirl of unending laughter and exciting challenges on and off the field, then blessings in ministry to a miraculous magnitude. It can only be explained as a mighty move of God. There have been bumps along the way, but even these have turned out to be growing points.

I've known times with friends who were hurting badly, moved by their ordeals to share all the bad things that have been lining up against them. But as the Bible says, Satan is "the accuser of the brethren" and "never keep account of evil." Some people have a mental list of all the bad things that have befallen them. Obsessing on problems simply draws in more problems. Just as faith is honored with answered prayers, dwelling on failure results in more failure. I have always tried to remind myself, when fighting Satan, to label it as a problem and run away. "Flee the very appearance of evil. Without faith it is impossible to please God" (Hebrews 11:6).

We must go back to the most basic attitude of the Christian faith. As the song says, "Count your many blessings; name them one by one and it will surprise you what the Lord has done." The more I count and recount, the deeper my gratitude grows. In many ways, the three weeks following that operation were the most awful I can remember, but also the greatest.

My survival was a miracle, made possible by thousands of prayers. This book is part of that miracle. It came as a result of just recounting all my blessings. Because I had a lot of time to think and pray, I came to feel more and more like a spoiled brat. Since so many people were praying for and loved me, but I could see suffering in the world (such as the earthquakes in Haiti and Chile) I think again, I am blessed beyond measure.

Everyone speaks of the importance of strengthening your core; diet and exercise is suggested. Touching your emotional and spiritual core is not so simple, but worth the exercise. Hopefully this book will help us to strengthen the core! The good, the bad, and the ugly must be admitted and honestly confronted—with concerted effort. "Lay back your ears."

Now, I blitz for the Lord. To give an example, I have made organizing "Weekends of Champions" an important part of my life's work. I'm always looking for a way to keep the pressure on! What's preventing us from conducting "Weekends of Champions" in 400 prisons every year?

LIFETIME OF BLESSINGS

But in spite of my recent trials, my whole life has been blessed. I had a powerful, blessing father and an over-blessing mother, a hero older brother and a sensational baby sister—all sweet, loving, blessing people. My grandfather was a giant of a man in every way, a county judge unashamed to bless his kids and grandkids. I grew up marching in an entire parade of idealistic, committed Christians who blessed me continually. "Even the times that appeared to be bad turned out to be good" (Romans 8:28).

However, all defensive coaches will admit, "You live by the blitz, but you can also die by the blitz." There are fewer men in the coverage and someone is going to be wide open.

The result is a cheap touchdown! Sensing that the all-out blitz is coming, the quarterback can call an audible at the line. That's what is called "checking the blitz." The new play is a dump-off pass to the tight end, who rumbles 50 yards down field and scores untouched. Or he could dump the pass off to a back flaring out of the backfield, and once more the defense is in trouble because the all-out blitz leaves no one to cover him. Again, this is a big gamble: "You live by it and you die by it." Blitzing all the time is an admission that you have a weak defensive line, because the front four really should be able to apply pressure on the quarterback without blitzing help. Even if their sack total isn't great, they should still be able to hurry the quarterback, so he doesn't have time to pick out his second or third receiver.

Any defense with an impressive sack total will have an even greater number of "first forces." That's football talk for defensive pressure that comes close to a sack. Often this is just as helpful. Your "first force" may hurry the throw and cause an interception. (A lot is discussed in Chapter Five by Paul Wiggin, my teammate and fellow Browns defensive end, about the rule change called "in the grasp," which made it easier for rushers to get the sack.) A lot of sack totals were improved by this rule, to protect quarterbacks.

I spoke earlier about the strong and loving people who surrounded me in childhood. One of those early blessings came to an end when I was 14 and my father died. To lose Dad caused a huge hole in the very core of my being. I then regained it through substitute fathers. The contrast between having and not having a strong father is so very clear to me when I see the lack of blessing in prison. The most violent criminals complain of abusive fathers. The damage to their emotional and spiritual core is almost always devastating. The results are a life of crime, drug abuse and insecurity, largely due to a father problem. Of course, in prison the damage is usually worse, but even in the free world there are many of us who haven't become terrorists or criminals, and yet have suffered untold "core damage."

That's why I feel so unusually blessed to have lived in a constant blitz of blessings.

CHAPTER 1

GROWING UP - EARLY YEARS

GROWING UP IN BLOOMBERG

The first five years of my life were spent in a little town in far northeast Texas called Bloomberg, population 500. The closest town of any size was Texarkana, 30 miles north. That's where I was born—it was the closest hospital. Driving into Bloomberg from Texarkana, your last few miles of road were paved with gravel. This continued through town and another eight miles all the way to the Red River, which marks the border between Texas and Arkansas. Everybody knew everybody and the whole town aided in the parenting of the children. "I'm gonna tell your Daddy what you're doing," or "Your momma will hear about this," were the everyday warnings you heard. But the kind words were just as plentiful, if not more so: "You are getting so big," or "You sure are stout (strong)." Hugs and kisses came freely and there was no abuse of kids or crime to speak of.

All adults seemed to be the "morality police," wanting to teach Bloomberg kids good values. Even those who were not Christians seemed to value honesty and other Christian virtues. No one questioned Christian morals. Even when someone would rationalize their behavior, finding some excuse for not living up to moral standards, no one asked, "What's wrong with adultery?" Nobody ever said, "At times you have to tell a lie." They never attacked the moral standard the way people do today.

My hometown was a warm and loving place to grow up. I was always called "William" by my family. My mother insisted that William was my name, not Bill or, as my big brother called me, "Willie." I really was never known as Bill until my high school coach, Bill Stages, renamed me after himself.

I had adoring parents and a hero of an older brother, who kicked me around a little, but would defend me against any outsiders. Cousins had "big brother rights" to protect me, just like my brother Vernon—unless, for some reason, they overstepped their rights and my big brother would put even cousins in their place. I liked it—I mean the whole small town system.

My mother and dad had both grown up there. There was a brother and sister on Dad's side and five brothers and two sisters on Mother's side. So there were many aunts and uncles who were always overly affirming and fun to be around. They took great interest in me, always bragged about me and built me up, pointing out my good character traits. I never remember one negative word from them. My cousins were great playmates. When we fought, it was more like sibling rivalries, than a fight between cousins.

We moved to Corpus Christi when I was five, but visited Bloomberg for at least a week or two every year and those aunts and uncles and cousins visited us in Corpus yearly, as well.

I'll never forget the day we moved out. Dad had what they called a general mercantile store. It carried everything you might need, in big quantities—feed, hardware, clothing, meats, groceries and building supplies. Along with the store, the operation also included a cotton gin and several warehouses, around back. There was even a blacksmith's shop on the property, which another uncle ran. I would watch for hours as he pumped his bellows to make the coal fire even hotter in order to heat the metal to a red glow. Then he'd beat it into whatever shape was called for. His face and hands were black from the coal, but he always told me interesting stories.

Dad's huge store was heated by a mammoth pot belly stove. Many an hour I sat in the warmth of it, on a five-gallon paint bucket I used as a stool. Around me were the older men of the town, and a few of the younger ones, sharing their intriguing stories. I could tell when a story wasn't altogether true, because my Dad would roll his eyes. When a story was just partly embellished he would roll his eyes a little less. He always indicated to me the truthfulness of a tale by the way he reacted. If the story was laced with too much vulgarity, he would clear his throat and look at the man, as if to say, "No cussing around my son!" It's been too long to recall details of what the men said. But I do remember that, at a dramatic point in the story, they would pause to spit tobacco juice on the pot belly stove. It would sizzle, as if to add an exclamation point. At times I couldn't help but ask questions, which they always tried to answer with enthusiasm. I was a good, and new audience for them.

We took our vacations in Corpus Christi and often thought how wonderful it would be to live in this beautiful city on the Gulf of Mexico. My dad loved to fish, and this was both a fisherman's paradise and a thriving business community. Sensing opportunity, Dad sold the Bloomberg store to his brother-in-law and became partners (with another brother-in-law, Herbert Alexander) in a Corpus Christi insurance and loan agency. This was a timely decision. Even in the early 1940s the city was growing, and of course when the Second World War ended, things heated up more. There was a steady stream of returning soldiers, most of them wanting loans and insurance policies for their homes, cars, and life.

With a population of 100,000, Corpus Christi was a far cry from Bloomberg, but it was still a great place to grow up. I could pedal my bike all over town, even ride the two miles out to Six Points, a neighborhood shopping and business area, or downtown to the movies, or to the beach and harbor, a distance of five miles. On warm days we went fishing or swimming in the bay. Even at 10 years old, I was free to roam all over town. I often went with Vernon (my older brother by seven years, whom family members called "Son") to fish or whatever he may be doing. Other times I'd head off with my friend Jackie Trice, who lived across the street.

It was during World War II, 1940 to 1945, that my Dad and I became friendly with a hot tamale vendor. You could find him every day by the drawbridge at the entrance to Corpus Christi Harbor. He sold his tamales out of a bike with a cart attached to its front, like an ice cream cart. The front box was maybe four feet square with an insulated compartment for the ice cream or, in his case, tamales. Dad and I often noted what a great location our friendly tamale man had chosen. When the bridge was up to let ships enter or exit the harbor, cars would be backed up for a long wait. It was a great time to sell hot tamales—people had nothing else to do.

During those war years we bought hot tamales at least once a week from this little man. In early 1945, with the war close to an end, our tamale vendor made headlines in the *Corpus Christi Caller Times*. I was 10 years old at the time, looking in disbelief at his picture on the front page. Turned out he was a German spy! It was discovered that he had a short-wave radio in a secret compartment of his cart, beneath the hot tamales. He was radioing all the shipping information concerning traffic in and out of this busy harbor, to submarines just off of our coast in the Gulf of Mexico. The subs would then transmit that info to the high command back to Germany. So now we knew how those submarines were able to sink so many of our ships transporting men and equipment to the war effort. I was intrigued as a young boy: My Dad and I actually knew a real live German spy!

I had a second spine-tingling experience that year, out on the Oso golf course with the big boys – my brother, Son, and his teammates on the Corpus Christi High School football team. They had decided to wade in the waterholes to get golf balls. I was thrilled to be allowed to go with the high school football stars. I adored my brother and his friends. I didn't realize that we were actually stealing the golf balls from the water hazards—that is, until I heard a man yelling, "You boys get out of that waterhole!" And then to my horror, I heard him firing a shotgun and even heard the pellets hitting the water around us. It was just bird-shot, and he was too far away to hurt us, but it scared me.

We took off running at top speed, slowing down only to grab our clothes on the bank. Still in my underwear, I was running as fast as my 10 year old legs would carry me, but was falling far behind. Son grabbed one of my hands, and his friend, James Jeffery, grabbed the other. My feet were hitting the ground every two or three steps and then as they ran faster I realized my feet weren't hitting the ground at all. I was flying through the air with my arms outstretched between the star high school quarterback and the star running back. And these boys were really fast! They both went on to successful careers in college, Jeffery at Baylor and Son at Rice. That night I was just pleased they were fast enough to out run the guy with the shotgun.

We reached the car and pulled on our clothes, laughing nervously and thinking we'd gotten away clean. Then, to our dismay, headlights flashed on and a car motor started. One of the big boys said, "Oh no! It's the cops!"

Now I was really shaking with cold and fear. Why did I want to come with them? We were relieved to learn that it wasn't the cops after all—just teens parking on a lonely road, smooching. I was so frightened I'm sure I wet my already wet pants. I was warned within an inch of my life to never tell anyone. I didn't for 60 years— until now. Since they are all dead, I don't guess it hurts to tell. Jeff and Son later laughed about me flying through the air, feet not touching the ground, especially since I ultimately weighed 270 pounds in top condition as a pro football player. Son and Jeff weighed no more that 170 or 180 pounds. Stealing golf balls, getting shot at—and almost caught—cured me of wanting to get in trouble with the law.

The golf course adventure ranks as my most frightening experience from those days. The most embarrassing was a year or so earlier, on the night I was introduced to Son's girlfriend, Marilyn. She had come to our house to meet our parents for the first time. The four of them—Son, Marilyn and my mother and dad were sitting in our den. While they were making conversation I was taking a shower, unaware of any expected visitors. I finished my shower, toweled myself off and was returning to my room through the den, stark naked. Son and Dad yelled in disbelief at my stupidity. I was so embarrassed that I just ran to my room, red-faced and unable to so much as look at Marilyn the rest of the evening. Well, that was the first time I met her, and little did I know she'd be the sweetest and most loving sister-in-law imaginable. I got off to an awful start, but things have gone great ever since. It's been over 60 years since then.

Since Son's death four years ago, I've tried to be there for her. She knows I've "got her back."

EARLY FOOTBALL

From the time I was six years old, I played constantly in the park across the street from our house. I went with the park, sort of like the swings and the tennis courts. Teenagers would let me play with them. It was always "full-speed tackle" football, played until dark every night. If there was an odd number of players, five on one team and six on the other, I would play on the team with five so it would be "fair and square." They always let me play and never seemed to take advantage of me being younger or smaller. Occasionally, they played baseball and I'd play too, but usually it was football. This was before I got slow and clumsy—a result of the growth spurt that left me athletically challenged. I was fairly fast and very competitive as a boy.

Football and baseball weren't my only sports. I learned to play tennis thanks to Obie Grief. He was my Dad's best friend and he and his family lived across the street. He taught me great technique—good enough to make me junior high doubles champion. That was thrilling, but I didn't continue playing in high school. Tennis is mastered through long hours of practice, and I never really applied myself.

Really, football was my only sport. Coach Bill Stages, another major influence in my life, taught me the fundamentals of defensive line play, and I kept returning to those fundamentals and was able to improve for the rest of my football playing years.

MY FATHER'S BLESSING

My earliest memories were of a father who sat on my bedside at night while we dreamed about my future and his. He was no sissy— a big, pro-baseball pitcher. He was very much a man, but freely gave his love and blessings with words of encouragement. Hugs and kisses came freely between him and his children, wife, and in a lesser way to everyone else. A "tuck me in" blessing which he bestowed on me most nights before I slept, buried itself deep within me and has never left. But when he died at age 45—when I was just 14—I was left with no one to bless me and it left a huge hole in my heart. At times, I thought I would also die, or at least I wanted to.

PRO-SIZED GENES

On both my mother and father's side of the family there was only one possible source for the DNA that produced a 6'6", 270-pound, pro-sized defensive end, and that was my grandfather on my dad's side. But God has been at work since the dawn of creation to make all things work together to produce His will. So it's really no big deal for Him to slide just the right genes my way, making it possible for sports to build me a platform from which I could make an impact for Christ.

I remember my grandfather well. He was a hulk of a man, a county judge and a landowner. He carried a gruff exterior, but he was a loving, sweet soul. He thought it was the sign of a real man to be totally honest, loving, and willing to express caring emotions. He died when I was only six, but I knew him well because my dad was just like him; to know one was to know the other.

MY GRANNY'S BLESSING

My Granny read to me for hours from her well-worn Bible. Amazingly, I was never bored sitting in her lap, or as I got older, in a chair by her side. She was my mother's mother, the most loving, sweet and humble woman I ever knew. She'd come live with us for a month or more in Corpus Christi every year, and I always looked forward to her visits. She would sit with us and play card games or tell stories of Indians she had befriended, or hobos she fed on her back porch in Bloomberg during the Great Depression, or of her husband who died working on the railroad in a train accident. She often spoke of rearing her children (five boys and three girls) alone after his death.

Granny was the best cook ever. Her pies were to die for, but everything she cooked was fantastic! Mother complained that she had no written recipes. It was just a pinch of this and a dash of that. Mother actually thought she was making sure not to create a written record of her recipes in order to retain the "Best Cook" title. But she was honest, genuine, hard-working, and loved God! All her children turned out to be hard-working, God loving, small-town solid citizens. When she read the Bible, she made it come alive. It was obvious she knew the author well. She was the female version of John Wooden, the great UCLA coach. It was Wooden who said: "Reputation is what people think you are and character is what you really are. Obviously, the most important thing is character." Granny had real character. She was a great woman of undeniable character. Paw-Paw Glass and Granny Endsley were so very important in my early life. He gave me my size and athletic ability. She gave me a hunger for God.

My life wasn't always blitzed by uninterrupted blessings. I was a very happy boy, until I hit the teen years. In fact, my early teens made me feel as if I was blitzed by a curse. Everything seemed to be conspiring against me.

My older brother was the star of the Corpus Christi High School football team. He was named All State and I was "all wet." I was a frustrated seventh-grader, the third-string quarterback on our junior high team. So no, it wasn't anything like the Manning brothers. When they saw that I was hopeless as a quarterback, they moved me to center, but I was even worse at that. I had three problems: I was too little, too slow, and too uncoordinated. Everybody expected me to be great like my brother, and I was anything but.

Corpus Christi was a football town. The stadium was packed with 12,000 to 15,000 fans for every Friday night game. I was a poor football player, and it was even tougher because I was Vernon Glass' little brother. I was a benchwarmer and really unhappy. I vividly remember sitting dejectedly on the bench during one of my junior high games.

To make matters even worse, my dad and his best friend Obie Grief were always big in the Quarterback Club. Obie was the host of a sports talk show on the radio and Dad and his partner were the sponsors through their insurance and loan agency called Alexander Glass.

In the game that I'm remembering we were winning easily but I was still stuck on the bench. An assistant coach sat down next to me and said, "I know how you feel, riding the bench in junior high. That's really the pits. But you must hang on to the feelings of this moment. It will be a great motivator for the future. You can say, 'I'll show 'em!' And when you grow and gain speed and coordination, you will use your 'I'll show 'em' attitude to become an even greater player than your brother."

I hung on every word because this was my first encouragement from a coach. He was a third-string coach, but from my point of view he was the head coach just saying what I needed to hear. I liked the "I'll show 'em" bit, even though to that point, I had nothing to show 'em except total football failure. I really didn't want to wait for that day in the far distant future when I would be bigger, faster, and more agile. When I looked in the mirror all I saw was acne and failure.

It was only made worse by the Quarterback Club, the radio show, the huge Friday night crowds at the football game, and the fact that the Glasses (father and first-born son) were the most prominent names in Corpus Christi sports. But the little brother was a misfit.

My dad knew I was depressed and tried to come to my aid by saying things like, "You don't have to play football like Son; I'll send you to any university you like." Son was getting football scholarship offers from every school in the country. I knew Dad was trying to make me feel better and I appreciated the effort, but it only confirmed what was becoming most obvious. I was a big disappointment to myself and everybody else.

Yes, I certainly felt that I was being blitzed not by blessings but by problems. I was hitting puberty; I had gone through a growth spurt that left me a klutz, athletically, with acne as a consolation prize. My parents and I went to the Second Baptist Church, a fundamentalist church that made me a social recluse. No dancing, no movies, no drinking, no mixed swimming (girls and boys together in a swimming pool) and whatever else was not even scripturally prohibited except by implication (maybe).

Then came Dad's Hodgkin's Disease.

I overheard Dad tell my mother about his Hodgkin's Disease for the first time. She cried during the discussion, but he tried to put the best face on it. "Dr. Moody says they are close to a cure for it, if I can just hang on for a couple of years, they will have a cure!" A cure was indeed discovered, though it was 20 years later instead of two. Either way, it was far too late for my Dad. Today people with Hodgkin's live a normal life span, which is wonderful. "I believe that God is going to cure me," Dad would say. "I've marked every passage in my Bible where God promises healing. They can give me treatments, which will arrest the symptoms," he reasoned.

He did keep up a good front around mother and me, but he was losing weight. Normally 205 pounds, he shrank down to 140 and looked painfully thin. His joints were losing lubrication and were extremely painful. Hot towels seemed to help and I filled the bath tub with hot water and soaked towels, which I kept coming in a constant stream. I'd burn my hands to get them hotter and he'd brag about me. "William gets them hotter than anyone!" It made me proud.

My Dad's sickness was an all-consuming thing. I soon forgot about my acne, my football, my schooling, and even my faith. I prayed that God would heal my Dad. But he only got worse. Bringing hot towels was my great mission. They provided his only relief from unremitting pain. It was also the only thing I could do to help. Like Dad said, "The Best!"

My normal development was put on hold for two years. I was stuck between a 12 year old and a teenager. I knew Dad was dying and nothing else was worth thinking about.

Son was now at Rice, making a big name for himself. I was so very proud to be his brother. He was my only claim to fame. I was never jealous. His success was my success. When Corpus Christi High School lost, I was sad for Son's sake. When they won, I was thrilled, and when he went to Rice, the family drove to Houston for every home game. Marilyn usually went with us and she would yell and cry if we won or lost. Everyone knew they would marry after Son graduated, and they did. I was delighted. But that happiness was saved for later.

The first summer after we learned about Dad's Hodgkin's, we went on a vacation to Colorado Springs. Mother, Linda (my baby sister, who was only one year old), Dad, and I rented an apartment on the edge of town. Son had a summer job with an oil company and didn't go on the vacation with us.

We did all the tourist things for the entire week of our "last vacation." No one called it the "last vacation," but everyone knew it probably was. We did all the activities on the brochures, like driving to the top of Pike's Peak (one of the tallest mountains in Colorado). We actually saw snow for the first time on its upper parts. We visited the Garden of the Gods, Seven Falls, The Cave of the Winds and good restaurants, like all good tourists!

The highlight of the vacation was a fishing trip with Dad. We drove about 60 miles north of Colorado Springs to Eleven Mile Canyon. I remember it like it was yesterday, even though six decades have passed. The Eleven Mile Canyon was, as it says, a long canyon with sheer cliffs, several hundred feet straight up, with a narrow road. Where the canyon walls were too narrow for the road to be squeezed between the little river and the cliffs, they blasted small tunnels through solid rock. The tunnels weren't very long, maybe 100 or 200 feet. The road was paved with gravel and wash-boarded from constant car and truck traffic. There was not a lot of traffic that day, and we were able to pull off the road and stop to fish a while.

We had bought a movie camera. It was an 8mm and Dad taught me how to use it. We took beautiful home movies of that magic day. We were very excited about having a movie camera: No one else I knew had one. I caught a mountain trout and Dad took a picture of me, proudly displaying my big catch. I was laughing and wiggling the fish right up close to the camera. Fortunately, that great day is still on film in our home-movie archive. As crude as those early films were, they are a treasure of the early and last memories of Dad.

We saw eagles gliding overhead and explored all 11 miles of the canyon. We stayed all day and had a picnic lunch Mother packed for us. As the sun was setting, we started for Colorado Springs, back through the dark tunnels and over the washboard road to its end where it rejoined the highway and went back into town.

At the end of the canyon, as we turned on the highway toward town, we came upon this quaint place called (at least in my memory) the Log Cabin Café. Dad said, "I'll bet you'd like some apple pie!" I agreed that would be great. Dad had a way of making even apple pie exciting. We stormed into the Log Cabin Café with a lot of laughter and fun. My Dad and I sat at the counter of the café and we were the only customers. So my Dad enthusiastically told the lady who was the cook, waitress, owner, and cashier all in one, about our day. "My son and I have just had the time of our lives; we spent most of the day up Eleven Mile Canyon watching eagles, fishing, and picnicking. It's got to be the most beautiful place on earth. We're from Corpus Christi in south Texas and that area is so flat. Oh, we have the Gulf of Mexico and great fishing, but this is a totally different world. The mountains and the sheer cliffs and the beautiful little river… it's just so different!

"Now, ma'am, I'm just wondering if you might happen to have any apple pie. It would be a perfect way to cap off a wonderful day!"

The lady had picked up on our excitement. She announced loudly, "Well sir, it so happens that I just pulled the most beautiful apple pie out of the oven. If I do say so myself, I make the best apple pie anywhere in these mountains."

My Dad interrupted, "I can't wait to dig into that pie and I know William here can eat a big piece, or maybe two. As you can see, he is a fine young man with a big appetite. This boy can really eat!"

Then he turned his volume down to a loud whisper and explained: "Now ma'am, I hope you won't think it's too much trouble and I know I'm kind of particular, but you wouldn't happen to have a slice of cheese? Not a thick piece, just a thin slice, that you could place on top of that large slice of pie, and put it back in the oven for a minute, just enough for the cheese to begin to melt. That would make it perfect!" The lady by this time was caught up in the excitement Dad had generated, about how we wanted to cap off the perfect day. Perhaps, in his mind, he knew this may be one of his last days with his son—just the two of us, in this heavenly place.

She exclaimed, "Sir, it just so happens that I know exactly what you want and I can do exactly what you and your hungry son have asked for."

"Well, you made our day," he replied.

That was the best apple pie I ever ate. Or, was it just the whole experience? What a fantastic day! On the way back to Colorado Springs, we drove through a wild electrical storm. The lightning would crack and the thunder boomed as if to place a huge exclamation mark on the end of that great day. It only added to my excitement! The whole day sizzled like the tobacco juice on the pot belly stove in that General Mercantile store in Bloomberg. The lightning strikes were like punctuation marks told in those stories at Dad's old store.

The next day, we began our trip back home—back to school and the business of daily life. Watching Dad's painful decline was agonizing!

DAD DIED

An even more vivid memory was that bleak day when they came to my junior high to pull me out of my class to tell me Dad had died. Everyone from Dad's circle of close friends was very supportive, and offered to take me fishing like Dad did. My uncle Weldon had moved to Corpus to take my Dad's place in the Insurance and Loan Agency where my uncle, Herbert Alexander (Dad's sister's husband), and Dad had built a thriving business in the middle of the post-War construction boom. The business had grown to the point where it was too much for my uncle to run by himself. So an arrangement was made. My dad's brother would come down to Corpus from Texarkana where he lived, and would help in the business. It was really good that it worked out that way, because all my dad's friends never got around to the promised fishing trips. I seldom saw them and they seemed too busy to spend time with me. But my uncle Weldon would come over to our house every evening after supper and sit and talk or play a spelling game called ghost. He was a different kind of man than my father, but he had a great stability about him that gave my mother and me, and I'm sure my two-year-old sister Linda, a feeling of well-being.

When I was overcome with the sadness of losing my Dad, two great things comforted me. First, you really haven't lost anyone if you know exactly where they are. Second, I thought very often of Dad's ordeal—how his aching joints would cause him to beg for hot towels, which seemed to help a little. But now, for the first time in two years, he was totally pain-free. He was in Heaven and supremely happy. He was eating apple pie with a thin slice of cheese, slightly melted. It was far better than at the Log Cabin Café.

I've often longed to join him in the heavenly version of the Log Cabin Café up Eleven Mile Canyon. I know it will taste and smell and look infinitely better than the earth-bound copy. All our human senses will be sharpened and perhaps we'll have a bunch of heavenly senses that will heighten the joy even more. Randy Alcorn in his classic book *Heaven* presents that possibility convincingly!

REVISITING ELEVEN MILE CANYON

I told my wife, Mavis, that last-vacation story so often that we decided to revisit the Eleven Mile Canyon on a vacation 40 years later. I went with the expectation that it would be nothing like the place in my memories—given that I was 13 at the time and under the stress of seeing my father shrink away to a skeleton of his former self. It couldn't be the fairy tale place I had remembered. But I was surprised to find that the tunnels, the little river, the sheer cliffs, even the eagles and the washboard road, were all exactly the same. Mavis and I packed a picnic lunch and sat on a huge flat bolder, facing the edge of the wild little river. We laughed and talked for a long hour. We explored all eleven miles of the canyon, just as Dad and I had done so long before. We watched an eagle poised on a big rock and saw it gracefully soaring to the top of the cliffs, hundreds of feet up into the clouds, they were the decandents of the very ones Dad and I watched forty years ago. We watched rock climbers scaling up an impossibly sheer cliff. They had more guts than sense, but it was fun to watch.

Then, late in the afternoon, we drove back through the narrow rock tunnels and along the washboard road. As we came to the highway going back to town, I was surprised to see the old log café was still there and I had to stop to show Mavis.

It was just as I had remembered. A long counter with small tables clustered in every corner of a large room. Again, we were the only customers and one middle-aged woman handled every job from cook to cashier.

I said, "Ma'am, my dad and I came to Eleven Mile Canyon 40 years ago, and we had the most wonderful day capped off with the best apple pie I ever tasted. It was in this very café. It might have been your mother. Who was the cook back then? Would you by any chance have any apple pie?"

"Well, sir," she announced, "it just so happens that I just took an apple pie I made myself, out of the oven not five minutes ago."

I warmed to the task. "Ma'am, you wouldn't happen to have a thin slice of cheese that you could place on top of a piece of that pie and let the cheese melt slightly for one minute in your oven, could you?" "Oh yes sir, I do," she shouted from the other end of the counter. That was the best piece of pie I had ever tasted, except the piece I had 40 years before with my dad.

CHAPTER 2

HIGH SCHOOL

MY COACH'S BLESSING

I was rescued from my depression over my dad's death by my high school coach, Bill Stages. He grew up in the Masonic Home in Fort Worth. His parents had died in a car crash when he was an infant. He knew what it was like to grow up without a mother or a father.

So he stepped in to fill the gap. Oh, he never said, "I want to fill the void left by your father's death," but he couldn't have done it more effectively with an earned doctorate in clinical psychology. He approached me matter-of-factly, simply saying, "I'd like you to stay after regular workout and work on your fundamentals with me."

He always used a drill that placed two football blocking dummies five yards apart with a big offensive tackle between and a little running back behind the lineman. He'd get me down in a good stance, facing the tackle, and yell instructions: "Back flat, head up, and head on a pivot. Fire into the tackle; never let him touch you between the knees and shoulders. Never let him get above you or beneath you. Stay in front of the block, hit 'em with your forearm and shoulder. Never go around the wrong side of the block. Shed the block and make the tackle!"

Then came my favorite part—he would walk back to the dressing room with his arm around me, constantly affirming my progress. He made me feel the way I felt when my dad rubbed my back. It gave me a wonderful feeling of "blessing." I didn't dread having to work after everyone else was in the dressing room taking a shower. I looked forward to it! It was like my dad was alive again!

I wondered why he wasted so much time on me. It's all right to be small if you also happen to be fast, but in sports when you're little and slow that is really bad. I was both! I guess he knew I would have to develop great technique to keep from getting killed. But, I went on to play for 22 years (10 in school and 12 in the pros). Later, my coaches in the NFL were the greatest coaches of all time: Don Shula and Paul Brown, who are both in the NFL Hall of Fame!

Shula was my first coach when I signed with the Detroit Lions. He was our defensive coordinator. He went on to Baltimore Colts and then to the Miami Dolphins where his team went undefeated, 17 straight victories. That's a record which may never be broken. Blanton Collier, my head coach at Cleveland for six of my seven years with the Browns, was to me the greatest football mind of all time. He should be in the Hall of Fame, also.

But I learned the basics from Bill Stages. He taught me things I never learned from those great coaches in the NFL. We weren't just coach and player. We were father and son. It was never said out loud, but understood and even communicated in non-verbal ways.

Every day at noon we lifted weights together down in a basement weight room, just the two of us. He'd sit beside me on the bus going out to the games, whether they were across town at the high school stadium, where we played our home games or way down the road by bus in San Antonio or Houston.

I later asked Fred Morgan, my close friend and teammate throughout our school years, if the other players understood what was happening. He assured me that they did, but liked it that Coach was trying to help make up for what I had lost.

Coach Stages was not a perfect man, but we came together at the point of both of our needs. There was magic in the blessing he bestowed on me. It affected my deepest insecurity; I needed to have a father's blessing.

He even renamed me. My mother had always insisted that my name was William, but Coach Stages said, "Your name is not William. We don't want you to be 'sweet William.' Your name is Bill." I always felt that he named me after himself.

"Your name is Bill!" he shouted.

"Yes, sir!" I replied.

MY MOTHER'S BLESSING

Oh, I had a super mother who, if anything, overdid the blessing. After our high school games, when the fathers lined up outside our dressing room to congratulate their sons, my mom was always there, waiting down the driveway from the dressing room with my sweet baby sister, Linda, 12 years younger than me. But dads had a way of boisterously grabbing, hugging, yelling, kidding, smiling, and just being alive. "Dang it!" I just missed that.

I'm older and still do. This last month, I've faced death a couple of times and have only gratitude to have lived such a blessed life. I've been a Consensus All American, inducted into the College Football Hall of Fame, All-Pro four times, and part of the World Championship team in the last year before the first Super Bowl, and even in the Texas Sports Hall of Fame. But those are minor blessings, compared to marrying and living 53 years of bliss with my soul mate, Mavis, and having three great children and eight grandkids, all mature beyond their years. They compete in their own cute ways to outdo each other at being a blessing. Being founder of Champions for Life has also been a super blessing, but more about that is in the last few chapters of this book.

Halfway through my sophomore year in High School I was a starter, simply because Stages had taught me the basics. I was still not over my three problems: Being slow, small, and clumsy, but I had gained 60 pounds and four inches in height between my sophomore and junior year. More importantly, I gained agility and became more aggressive. I actually kept picking up weight, height, speed, and even athleticism into my late twenties. In high school, my top weight and height was 210 pounds, 6'3", and in college, 230 pounds, 6'5". Finally in the pro ranks I got up to 270 pounds and 6'6".

MORGAN HAD MY BACK

I've enjoyed 61 years of friendship with Fred Morgan. We played together as seventh-graders at Wynn Seale Junior High in Corpus Christi. I led him to the Lord during our years at W.B. Ray High School. He has served on our Board of Directors at Champions for

Life for many years; we vacation together, we serve Christ together, and we think a lot alike and are brutally honest with each other. It is never necessary to cushion a discussion with introductory thoughts to prepare a real friend like Fred. We go, at once, to the heart of the matter.

I let Fred read the first draft of this book in which I mused concerning Stages giving me so much time and attention and yet I couldn't remember anyone ever kidding me about it. On a team, these kinds of things never pass without someone saying something like, "brown-noser!"

He admitted, "Yeah, I can remember on more than one occasion hearing it discussed." But I'd say, "That's out of bounds. You guys know about his dad dying and how badly it hurt him. Coach Stages understands because he lost his parents as a baby and grew up in an orphanage, so just keep your mouth shut, and I'm serious!"

That is the cleaned-up version of his comments. I'm sure he actually used some of his pre-Christian language, but Fred never mentioned it to me until I questioned him about it. He remembered that it had been discussed and, in modern prison lingo, he "had my back." I ran interference for him when I was blocking on the line on that High School team. He ran interference for me with our teammates, and now does so as a Board member and close friend. We keep "firing out" for the greatest cause.

As I said in the first chapter, the one thing I regret about my High School years is growing up in a church that was too legalistic. To them, Christianity was a series of rules, most of which were not found in the Bible. I Corinthians 9 teaches that we should become "All things to all people." I had a lot of growing to do in order to relate to all types of people, even to those whose lifestyles were repugnant to me.

God tells us to bend, as far as, possible in order to "win the more!" The question is how far do we go and Paul tells us in this passage to be as flexible as possible, but not to go so far that you become a "castaway" and get into their sinful lifestyle. But he is saying go far enough so that you must guard against going too far and falling into their sins. It's obvious that Christians, then and now, tend to be rigid so he had to name five different groups that we must adapt to: the Jew, the weak, the ones under the law, the ones not having the law, and all things to all people.

An evangelist must be flexible and able to be "all things." But perhaps that church did me more good than I think. I found Christ there in Second Baptist Church – Corpus; I learned evangelism and I met friends, who are, to this day, close friends, and involved in Champions for Life. Paul Martin, one of the people I met there as a boy, comes to serve in Weekends of Champions often and is involved in the leadership of the Houston local team. I so respect this committed Christian attorney, whom I came to know back there in that funda-mentalist church.

I took Fred Morgan with me to that church and it was there that he came to Christ. I was told by the Pastor, Warren Walker, that anyone I won to Christ could be a part of my Sunday school class. I ended up having the biggest class in the church— more than 150 members. They were all different ages, some male and some female. I had a lot of fire, but not much knowledge. Leading people to Christ gave me a great thirst for learning the Bible. How could I answer their objections without the right scripture? I memorized most of the verses in the Bible that answered most of the questions anyone may have. Much of my class was teaching the plan of salvation and overcoming and answering objections of the lost in order to win them to the Lord. It was practical and simple. It had to be because I knew so very little. I did find a book that contained objections and answers. I drilled that book into my class Sunday after Sunday!

Many of my class members turned into fruitful Christians. Come to think about it, I owe a great deal to that church. Even my legalism was ultimately repented, but I managed to hold on to many of the positive things from that experience. I didn't have a strong church exposure until my late teens, so I was unaware of how different my class was—with its tendency to cut across age groups and find alternatives to regular Sunday school literature.

MY MOMENT OF SALVATION

I found Christ in a dynamic conversion experience at 16 years of age in Second Baptist. It was during a Sunday morning church service. I'd been going to that church for several years, but didn't know Christ.

Obie and Joy Grief, who lived across the street and who were our best friends, found Christ there and Dad did too. All the children tagged along. From the age of about 10, I went to church there, but didn't actually experience rebirth for many years. After my genuine conversion there was an immediate change in my life. I became intense about winning people to Christ. I took them to the pastor, I'd knock on his study door and say, "He's ready, lead him to Christ." For several months I'd bring people of all ages and types to him and he was always pleased and encouraging. I often brought in many at once.

But then one day, after speaking to someone I brought to Christ, he asked me to stay in his study for a talk. He said, "You know, Bill, you don't need me. You have watched and listened as I've led them to Christ for months now. You have won more people to Christ than anyone I know. Why not lead them through the plan of salvation yourself?" That frightened me! What if I did something wrong and they weren't genuinely saved? He assured me it was God who does the saving. I was to just show them the scriptural plan of salvation.

I had his plan of salvation almost memorized, having witnessed it so many times. He used the same plan every time. He was the surgeon and I was just the nurse. No doctor would turn to the nurse and say, "You've watched me so much you can just do the surgery without my help." But that was precisely what he was saying to me. I was hesitant, or perhaps I was again just seeking the father substitute. I loved his approval, but he was now sending me out on my own. Throwing me in the deep end of the pool, saying, "Sink or swim!"

He was much like Coach Stages, teaching me tackling. The coach would say, "They can't fake with their belt buckle. Now they can give you a head fake, or even a head and shoulder fake and you'll go for it, because you aren't watching their belt buckle. They can also fake with their feet, but just focus on the belt buckle. Fire your shoulder through their navel and they'll come down every time. But you must 'wrap out' and grab your own left wrist with your right hand, and 'lockout' with your arms, and go all the way around their waist with your shoulder buried into their core. Pull them into you and bury them into the ground." Stages repeated this speech loudly and over and over and over!

Now you would think no one ever made a tackle any other way. But, in a game he didn't care: "Just get 'em down, clothesline 'em, grab any part of their body and get 'em on the ground." But if you miss the tackle it was back to the basics. "You didn't lock out, you didn't focus on the belt buckle," he'd repeat.

It is exactly the same way with a good witness. You'd think the only way anyone ever comes to Christ is via "The Roman Road," "Evangelism Explosion," "Four Laws," or whatever plan of salvation is their favorite. Mess with anything, but not their plan of salvation. That which you repeat under pressure tends to groove itself into permanence.

I've noticed that when someone says there are many ways to lead a person to the Lord, they tend not to do it often. When they lock in on one plan of salvation it tends to get grooved in their mind and they become really professional at its use. There are many different approaches depending on the needs of the person you are talking to. This is where you must be adaptable. If you are talking to a Muslim don't criticize their faith. Often, they became a Muslim for protection in the prison and aren't true believers. If you are a Republican, forget political arguments when talking to a Democrat. If you are on Death Row, forget discussions of capital punishment. But when they are ready to trust Christ, use the plan of salvation that you have grooved in your heart and mind!

So I moved reluctantly from operating room nurse to surgeon. God's plan in the New Testament is for everyone to be the surgeon. Everyone should be sharing the plan of salvation because "faith comes by hearing and hearing by the word of God" (Romans 10:16). We often tend to think it's the pastors or the evangelists who are to win the lost to Christ. In Ephesians 4:10-13, Christian leaders are simply "equipping the saints," including all Christians, "to do the work of the ministry," which is first and foremost leading the lost to Christ. We have reversed this scriptural order and said it's the pastor's or evangelist's job to do the work of the ministry. In fact it is our job to enable or encourage the church leaders to do the ministry.

When a Christian withdraws from this basic task, he or she tends to become active in some other phase of Christianity that can be counterproductive, like anti-abortion protests, giving to churches so they don't have to personally serve (mercenaries, they're called), or throwing himself or herself into Bible studies, church attendance, praying, fundraising, gifts of the spirit, Second Coming debates, and many other worthy or even great causes. But these activities can be a substitute for the greatest purpose of any Christian: To be a witness to the lost.

As I said before and will say again in Chapter Nine, these side issues can make the non-Christians hate us and close the door to our leading them to Christ. So, we don't "win the more" as it says in I Corinthians 9. We need to keep this prime purpose so central that we will do almost anything to keep the door open (except fall into sin ourselves, I Corinthians 9:27 "and become a castaway").

In the Weekend of Champions, I am once again seeing "God at work." He was preparing me for the Weekend of Champions from the very beginning of my Christian growth. I've always been an evangelist. Whether it was escorting the lost to my pastor or later performing the delicate surgery myself, the thing that really fired me up was seeing the lost come to Christ. I'm certain that our most important task in Champions for Life is training Christians to share their faith. But, that's what I was doing in that first Sunday school class back in Corpus.

CHAPTER 3

BAYLOR

THE BLESSING OF BEING TOUGH

I did get a lot of football scholarship offers. I only wish Dad had lived to see it. I finally accepted one to Baylor University. At the end of my freshman year I was invited to dinner at Dr. White's house; he was the President of Baylor. Dr. Wimpee was his assistant, and was the one who arranged the dinner.

I was somewhat surprised by the direction of the conversation of the evening. The head coach at Baylor was George Sauer. He had complained to the President that Baylor could never be a winner in football because Christianity made our players too nice. We just weren't "mean" enough to make good players. I admitted to Dr. White and Dr. Wimpee that I had been working hard my whole football life against that false image of the timid Christian athlete. Even in high school I was criticized for not being "mean" enough by some people, but never by Coach Stages. He always seemed to point out how "tough and mean" I in fact was. He had stressed to me the importance of not being a nice guy on the field. I would think and repeat to myself, "not dirty," or "not a cheap-shot artist" as I went through drills and competition. Instead the simple idea was to be a tough hard competitor who never backed down. Years later when I played for the Browns, a *Cleveland Press* columnist, Frank Gibbons, wrote, "Everybody knows he is just as hard as the water from an old ranch well." I felt blitzed by the blessing of being a tough and even mean competitor.

Even as a freshman at Baylor I kept repeating to myself, "Stay up in their faces and hit harder than anyone!" I was playing middle guard on defense and the TCU coach complained that I had knocked out all three of their centers. I'm sure the opposing coach was exaggerating, but he did say it to a sportswriter who put it in the newspaper. I felt good to finally be known as something other than "not mean enough!"

I made it a point to clobber the center with a strong forearm and keep him off of my body and fight against pressure. If he tried to cut me off from going to my right, I knew that's the very place I must go to stop the play. He was trying to "wall me off" and stop my pursuit of the play and I couldn't allow him to be successful in that attempt. It's what coaches called "fighting pressure." But it all started with me hitting him hard enough to stand him up and offset whatever he was trying to get done.

So early in my freshman year at Baylor I gained a reputation of being a very tough player. That's why the administration wanted to talk to me, because I was a good counter-example to what Coach Sauer was trying to tell them. Dr. White asked the coach who was his toughest player and the coach had to admit I was among the toughest, as well as being the most outspoken Christian. Tim Tebow is a great current example of this today. He is a tough competitor and carries the fight to his opponents. As a Christian we must play with guts and gusto! Football is a platform, which is most strengthened by great play.

Football was important because it was something I enjoyed and did well. Since Coach Stages had taught me the basics, I learned to keep the blocker from ever getting to my body, keep him from getting lower than I was, and stay in front of the pressure. To keep good separation, you have to keep them away from your legs or body, so you can maneuver. I really was seldom blocked. If it happened, it was due to a lack of concentration on my part. For my whole football career I was still practicing the drill I learned in High School. That drill embodies almost everything you need to know about defensive line play. If you master the drill, you are set for life and are virtually unblockable.

IN TROUBLE

There was a tradition at Baylor for the upperclassmen to steal the freshman class president and take him to a remote location and leave him there. We were feeling our oats and decided we needed to play that game, too. So four freshmen – John Preston, a 6'5", 220 pound lineman, Charlie Bradshaw, a 6'8", 250 pound lineman (who would play at 300 pounds in the NFL), Dick Baker, a 200 pound back, and yours truly – put on raincoats and black hoods and stormed into Brooks Hall. We grabbed the sophomore class president and drove him five miles out into the country, leaving him there in his pajamas. By midnight, they had traced my license plates and we were caught red-handed.

We had to go before a disciplinary committee made up of professors, deans and coaches. We especially knew we were in trouble because the coaches were there. The four of us were part of the nucleus of the freshman football squad. The coaches didn't want to see us get kicked out of school.

The Dean of Students waxed eloquent on what a terrible thing we had done. He decided to get dramatic at one point and fired off a question.

"Just how did you make those hoods?" he shouted. He obviously didn't really want an answer. But Bradshaw launched into a long and detailed answer.

"Well, Dean," he drawled in his best East Texas accent, "It's just not that hard. You just cut you out a little square of cloth and you sew it up on both sides and the top. And, of course you'll need to cut you out some eye holes, a nose hole, and a mouth hole. And there you have you one, Dean, if you ever want to make you one; it's just not that hard." The truth is my own sweet mother had sewn them up on her electric sewing machine, thinking she was making us Halloween masks. (We didn't let the disciplinary committee in on that detail.)

The room, by this time, had broken into uproarious laughter, including professors, coaches, and everyone except the Dean. We were given 17 demerits and told to get out and stay out of trouble, and we did. For sure, my mother never found out how much trouble we got into.

Charlie Bradshaw was a respected Dallas attorney until he died in his late 60's of colon cancer. I was asked to preach at his funeral. I told the story about stealing the sophomore class president and how Charlie defused the situation with his amusing comments, thus reducing our punishment. I asked that all of the attorneys stand and say a word for Charlie. At least 100 of them stood and told brief stories, or just one-liners. To say the least, it was touching.

Then I asked that all the football players who had played with him at any level to stand and say a word for Charlie. I was amazed to see another 100 former teammates stand and speak brief but equally touching, words of tribute to Charlie. I only regretted that Ardean, his wife, wasn't there to hear it. She had died suddenly of a brain aneurism about a year earlier.

People were there from all over the country for Charlie's funeral. They came from his Baylor days, his NFL days and even his Center, Texas school days. His attorney son and lovely daughter were comforted by the outpouring of love and good humor. People were crying and laughing all afternoon, before and after the funeral. People didn't seem to want to leave. They hung around at the reception for over an hour. I certainly stayed to the last, because I was saying goodbye to a friend of 50 years. There are no friends like old friends!

We were teammates, went double on our first date with the women who would become our wives, and were groomsmen in each other's weddings. We were opponents in the NFL, but always close friends. He loved to debate any subject and at times our debates would get heated, but we'd end up with a hug, a back-slapping, or occasionally, a wrestling match. We broke a lot of glassware and furniture because we were huge and rough. He was brilliant in every way and disarmingly humorous with his East Texas logic and down-home wisdom.

SURPRISED BY BLESSING

I've expressed a lot in my books and motivational talks about goal-setting, but as I rack my brain and dig for the truth about my own personal blessings, and what some may call achievements, I admit they were always a surprise. My success usually did not come as a result of a goal-achieving process.

In December of my senior year, my head coach at Baylor called me to his office and asked, "I'm sure you know why I've asked you over to visit with me."

I struggled because I couldn't remember anything I'd done that he'd be disciplining me for. I'd been very careful to not get in any trouble since our theft of the sophomore class president three years earlier. "No sir, I can't imagine," I confessed.

He was tearing up; I'd never seen that before. He was reassuring me. "I've never coached a Consensus All-American," he finally said.

"Who could this be?" I asked. He hugged me and started crying. In those days, men didn't do a lot of hugging, and certainly not crying. I felt that "Father's blessing feeling" flood over me. It came out of nowhere, Dad, Stages, God—and now of all people, my Head Coach, Sam Boyd.

THE "ME TOO" BLESSING

When Mavis and I married we really didn't know each other that well. I know that a brief courtship is not the best marriage preparation—it comes down to making a lifelong commitment to someone you really don't know. But, again, God was blessing in the process. For months during our whirlwind courtship and early marriage we were astounded as to how many things we had in common. We were constantly saying, "Me too!"

Both of our mothers grew up fatherless. Their fathers died before they were four years old—both of them killed in train accidents. They remembered very little about their dads. Both of our mothers grew up in small East Texas towns, both in big families, and each of them was the baby of their family. They shared the experience of being raised by brothers and sisters and one parent. Both of these young ladies moved to south Texas shortly after marrying and raised their families there— my mother in Corpus Christi and hers in Harlingen. Whether it was a casual statement of unimportant preference, or a pivotal strong conviction, it seemed amazing how often our conclusion was, "Me too!" We had a small puppy and we named him "Me Too," simply because we seemed to be coming to that conclusion about everything. We were amazingly alike!

Obviously, the ideal courtship would be to seek and find one's soul mate, someone with whom you mainly agreed. But if this scenario could not be arrived at over years of getting to know each other, then perhaps God could arrange it supernaturally. And He did! The "Me Too" miracle ranks high on my list of obvious blitzed-by blessings. Each of us had a deep thirst for God – wishing to know Him better and to serve Him fully!

Mavis went steady with a young man in high school, which meant they dated no one else. Even when he went away to college at Rice, they dated no one else. He was a brilliant student and a good high school football player. They thought they were in love and would someday be married. But Mavis' parents insisted that she date other people when she went to Baylor. They didn't disapprove of her high school boyfriend; they just wanted her to be open to other people. I'm so glad they insisted on this as a condition of sending her off to school. Otherwise, I probably would never have met her.

THE MAVIS BLESSING

Everybody kept telling me about this gorgeous freshman who wanted to meet me. At first, it was just something to laugh about with friends. "She hasn't even seen me, and when she does, she'll be much less interested," I assured my buddies.

"No", they said, "she has a big picture of you from the Waco newspaper taped to her mirror. She tells everyone she is determined to meet you."

She later explained to me that when she came to Baylor she thought it would be a great Christian school. But she had been asked out on many dates by freshmen football players who had shown less than noble intentions. She was flattered by all the interest shown by the opposite sex, but, again, it was not the kind of attention she really wanted.

Then she read an article about a Baylor senior football player who taught a Sunday school class. He aggressively filled his class with freshman. His technique would be to clean out the freshmen men's dorm by flipping mattresses, rolling them abruptly to the floor and demanding that they be in his class in 15 minutes or else! They came at first out of fear, but they came in great numbers. They even grew to enjoy it.

Mavis Knapp was the beautiful freshman who read of Bill Glass and his roughhouse methods. She told friends and even her parents that she wanted to meet this guy. Maybe he would be able to show her how a real Christian gentleman ought to act. Her friends assured her that he would have no interest in her. They would soon see how wrong they were.

Every day at noon Baylor students would gather in the Union Building for what we called "Singspiration." It was more or less a Christian sing-a-long, attended by hundreds. It was a great place to see and be seen. It lasted only 30 minutes between morning and afternoon classes. After it was over the foyer was packed with students just talking. One day, a friend grabbed me by the arm and hustled me to an agreed meeting place while another friend delayed Mavis.

"Here he is," my friend said teasingly, "This is Bill Glass, the guy you told everyone you wanted to meet." Mavis was so embarrassed she simply said, "Hi!" and ran away. I was impressed at how beautiful she was, so I chased after her, to the delight and laughter of several match-makers in the crowd.

I caught up to her and politely asked for a date that Sunday. I said I would pick her up at her dorm at 10 a.m. I had to preach in a local church that morning, so I asked her if she'd like to take part in the church service. She seemed puzzled. I explained, "Can you sing or play an instrument?"

"Oh," she kidded, "I can play the harmonica!"

Anyway, we got off to a fast start! After church that morning, we went to a cafeteria for lunch. She had her tray stacked high with food. I looked and said, "You must be really hungry!"

She explained, "It all looked so good—and I've never been to a cafeteria," she said, blushing. I immediately regretted the foolish comment. Charlie Bradshaw and his girlfriend joined us for lunch. Fortunately, he came to my rescue with a funny comment. He said, "You know, one of the only things I don't like about Ardean (his girlfriend) is that when I buy her a good meal at a restaurant she eats it all. She should leave at least half of it for me!"

Charlie was a brilliant student. One of his law professors told me he was one of the best students who had ever gone through Baylor Law School. But his childhood in small-town Texas left its mark in many amusing ways.

A few weeks earlier, we took a long plane trip to play against the University of Miami. Charlie kept turning the light switch on and off in our Miami beach hotel room. I teased, "Charlie, haven't you ever seen a light switch?" He said, "Sure, since I came to Baylor." He lived so far out in the country that the utility lines stopped a half a mile short of his house. He studied with a coal oil lamp through high school, but it didn't seem to slow him down scholastically.

He could also read a social situation astutely, and he saved me at the cafeteria that day, making a joke on himself when he saw Mavis embarrassed. But I did notice that she left a lot for Charlie and me to clean up.

Soon, the pace of our lives picked up. I started being selected for the All-American teams, and had to travel to New York City more than once, to appear on television shows where they introduced the All-American team to the nation. It was surely a thrill to be on TV with Ed Sullivan and Perry Como, but it turned out that meeting the other All-Americans was the best part of the experience. Many of them would become good friends during our pro careers—including teammates like Jim Brown and opponents like John Brodie, Jerry Kramer, and Jim Parker. In those days, there were only eleven All–Americans named each year—who played offense and defense. Most turned out to be great NFL players, if not superstars.

By November, Mavis and I were on the front page of the Waco newspaper, sharing a malt with two straws, cheek to cheek, at Baylor Drug, across the street from the campus. Our love for each other was mentioned often in news coverage of my football career. By this point, her high school boyfriend must have known. So, at Christmas vacation her mother made her return his football letter jacket and other keepsakes. It was a tough assignment for her, accompanied by many tears and apologies. Breaking up is never easy! I respected him because he never pushed her sexually. That was important then and it should be now. Mavis and I were both virgins when we met. We did it God's way. That, too, was a blessing.

Soon the team went to New Orleans to play Tennessee in the Sugar Bowl. The Volunteers were ranked second in the nation. If we could beat them, we would move up in the national rankings ourselves. I was excited about the game, but even more excited about my new-found love with Mavis.

STREETCAR DATE

She traveled to the game by car with friends. On the eve of that Sugar Bowl, we went out together, on a streetcar date. I thought, "A nice quiet evening alone, just the two of us." But, to my dismay, plastered all over the streetcar were posters showing my picture. They were hyping the big game, spotlighting me as the Baylor All-American going up against Tennessee's All-America player, Johnny Majors, (who would go on to become a famous coach for Tennessee). Thankfully, no one noticed. We drank coffee in a quaint New Orleans cafe and enjoyed the atmosphere of our blossoming love in this romantic town.

As I've noted, our relationship found itself on the fast track right away, mainly because we were so compatible. On our first date, Mavis had amazed me by offering the matter-of-fact statement: "I want to marry someone just like you." I was shocked and uncertain about her honesty, and even her sanity. But, after our third date I was agreeing. Soon, we were planning out a June wedding. On November 1st, after our last game of the regular season, I drove to Harlingen to give her an engagement ring and meet the entire family.

Her mother had planned a huge party to announce the engagement. There were at least 75 people in their large home. Most of them were brothers, sisters, and cousins of Parker Knapp, Mavis' father. Her mother was a beautiful lady, an older version of Mavis. The party was on a Sunday evening after church where I preached in the First Baptist Harlingen. I noticed my future father-in-law in the audience with his arm around another woman. For the first time, I felt uncomfortable about Mavis' family. Why was he with this stranger?

Later in the service, I noticed on the opposite side of the church, he had moved and was sitting beside his wife. I did a double-take back to where I had seen him before, and there he was again with his arm around the strange woman!

Of course I later discovered that he had an identical twin, Gilson Knapp, who was also his business partner. The twins' two older brothers, Everett and Johnny, were also present, sitting with their wives, children and grandchildren. They were 20 years older and had started the business 20 years earlier. They owned five Chevrolet dealerships in Brownsville, Harlingen, Mercedes, Weslaco, and Houston. They also owned a bank, canning plant, and 3,000 acres of orchards and a hunting ranch. Fredrick, the youngest of the five brothers, wasn't there because he managed the Houston dealership.

At the party on Sunday night at Mavis' parent's home, the eldest brother, Everett, the undisputed boss of the partnership of the supposedly equal partners, shocked everyone. Quite matter-of-factly, he told everyone that he had been so impressed with my sermon that he almost went forward during the invitation. He only held himself back because he was Episcopalian and didn't know if he would fit in among members of a Baptist church. To have Everett say what he said was quite a blessing for me. I'd received the stamp of approval from the patriarch of the Knapp family. Mavis had told me in advance that I shouldn't expect to receive approval quickly and especially not from Everett, who was a good man, but who reserved judgment. Yet he freely spoke his mind. I couldn't have been any more blitzed by blessing.

What a beautiful family and lovely home! Her mother, also named Mavis, was gorgeous. Our daughter and granddaughter carry the name Mavis as well, to the 3rd and 4th generations with all of it's looks and class.

On the father's side, the family was well to do and well-educated, mainly at Texas A&M. Her mothers' family was more country, small town, uneducated, but solid and down-to-earth, also more dedicated Christians. My family was exactly the same. But there were no losers on either side for generations especially humble, fine people. Far from perfect, but I wasn't ashamed of any of them. In fact, I was honored to claim kin to all of them! Obviously, I'm sure that God alone is the real judge.

I was feeling great, believing I had made a real hit with the family, until the next morning when Mavis' 11 year old sister, Gretchen, put me in my place. She grabbed hold of my biceps and said, "You are just such a big, sexy man!" I was amazed that this 11year old (mature enough to be 16) would act so flirtatiously. But then she came to her real point, saying, "You need some deodorant; you have B.O.!"

Mavis, I neglected to mention, has no sense of smell. When she was 12 years old she was thrown from a horse and knocked unconscious for two weeks before finally coming to. She recovered completely, except she never regained her ability to smell. She was also left with chronic back pain. I have to be mindful about using deodorant and breath mints because she can't warn me of odors. But Gretchen was kidding me about the body odor, I guess. She was constantly kidding me and keeping me on my toes about everything!

I'd signed to play my first professional season in the Canadian Football League. I had also signed a contract to do a television ad with "Pure Milk," a milk company out of Waco. They paid me $500 to appear in the ad. I made $14,000 with the Saskatchewan Rough Riders that first year. They gave me a $2,000 signing bonus. I thought I was rich! What a deal! They had paid me to do something I loved doing— play football.

A Consensus All-American, first draft choice for Detroit and Saskatchewan, Canada, and I only made $14,000. But in those days, it was a lot of money. Today I would make millions, but I was just as happy as the spoiled millionaires of today. I say more power to them. Many of them seem to figure out stupid ways to mess up their lives anyway. Thank God for a lot of other ones like Tebow, who are solid Christians.

In Canada, I didn't have to play on Sunday, which, at that point in my Christian life, would have been a real obstacle, because I was legalistic.

With all this money in my pocket, I knew I could support my lovely new wife, but in that romantic New Orleans atmosphere, our big problem became how to make ourselves wait until June. We were both virgins and were determined to stay pure until we were married. I asked, "Why don't we get married during our spring break?" She said, "Why not?" So our wedding date was pushed up to March 2, 1957.

THE BLESSING OF PEACE AFTER A SUGAR BOWL VICTORY

The Sugar Bowl was a great victory! We beat Tennessee soundly. I was the kicker on the opening kickoff, I caught the ball just right, with the wind to my back and it sailed high above the goal post and deep into the end zone bleachers. The crowd went wild and we never looked back.

What an end to a great season! Beating the number two team in the nation, and convincingly! My great kickoff wasn't actually that important, except that it was the start of a great game that kept getting better all day long. Except for one unfortunate play, the game was perfect!

After the game, I went over to the Tennessee dressing room to apologize on behalf of our team. In the heat of the battle, one of our players had lost his temper and kicked a Tennessee player in the head. It was an ugly scene. Their player was kicking and jerking and appeared to have suffered a terrible brain injury. After the game he was just fine. But, at the time it was a real "bummer" in an otherwise great day.

The Tennessee coaches and players were very appreciative of my gesture. I even met Frank Clement, the Tennessee Governor, who happened to be in the dressing room. Our paths would cross again later. All I remember was his appreciation for the apology. Again, what blessings I was receiving, at my young age of 21! Even to fill the role as a team leader of asking forgiveness for my teammate was an important duty! Our player who lost his temper suffered a great deal more than his victim! It took him many years, just to forgive himself. He was actually a fine guy, who became a wonderful man, but in that one situation he had lost control and acted out.

It had been only a few short years since my miseries as bench warming quarterback on the third string of a junior high team. I had, as the coach suggested, been using my "I'll show 'em" attitude to put "fire in my tail" and keep driving for victories. They seemed to come easier as I continued developing speed and agility and kept improving my technique. As for motivation, I simply call up that mental image of sitting on that bench years earlier. Immediately the "I'll show 'em" anger would rise up within me.

How had all this progress unfolded? I can answer that by describing something even more influential than the instruction and urgings of Coach Stages. It was an unforgettable prayer meeting I had with a friend named Larry Walker. It took place before my senior year of college. Larry made a frank statement to me one day, saying that despite my success I wasn't living up to my potential. He enthused, "You could be an All-American." I had not even imagined such a thing. I was just satisfied to be a starter. He said, "Let's pray," and suggested that we take

Matthew 18:19 for our inspiration. "I tell you that if two of you on earth agree about anything you ask for, it will be done for you by my Father in heaven."

So we got down on our knees and prayed fervently, claiming that promise. We agreed as it said that I would become an All-American and use football as a platform, to share my faith every time I could. We could feel God's presence in the room and knew something great would happen.

We went to California to play USC that first week of the season. I was expecting God to bless my actions on the field. Sure enough, I surprised even myself. I made 17 unassisted tackles and 10 assisted tackles. I was playing middle guard on defense and made tackles on both sides of the field. I would fire into the center and slide down the line to make the tackle. It was amazing: One play, I tackled what I thought was a faking ball carrier, but it turned out he'd actually had the ball. I could feel the "I'll show 'em" motivation, but even more, I sensed God was at work, and I was playing far above my natural ability. I knew God was answering that Matthew 18:19 promise.

Our next game was against the University of Maryland, a road trip to the East Coast. I couldn't believe it, but the USC experience basically replayed itself. One play in particular stands out. Our great punter, Delbert Shofner, who later played in the NFL for many years with the New York Giants and the Los Angeles Rams, kicked the ball 70 yards and very high. I was the deep punt center. After snapping the ball, I ran top speed and arrived at the punt receiver only a split second after he fielded the ball. I hit him chest high and buried my shoulder into him. The ball popped out and we recovered, setting up our winning touchdown.

After winning games on the West Coast and East Coast, we traveled to the Heartland to play, Nebraska. Again, I had a dominating game. By now, we were starting to play conference games in the Southwest Conference, which was a highly respected league at the time.

Our sports information director was a great guy named Wright who had held the Sports Information Director position at Rice when Vernon was their quarterback. He really liked Vernon and transferred those feelings to me. Vernon didn't get a fair deal at Rice because he was second string behind Tobin Rote. According to Wright, and most everyone else, he was a better quarterback. He wasn't a starter until his senior year after Rote had graduated. I always felt he was trying to make up for the raw deal Vernon got at Rice by favoring me.

He explained to me after the season, "You had three great games early in the season—on both coasts and then in the Midwest. That exposed you to more sportswriters of influence than you'll be seen by in the rest of your games combined! You really had a lock on your All-American honors after the third game. Of course, you had to continue to play well in conference play and you did, but you were lucky that the schedule exposed you to all those writers early."

It didn't hurt that our publicity director was always giving me the benefit of the doubt. Hal Wingo was the sports editor of the *Baylor Lariat*, our school newspaper. It was his job to keep track of who did what statistically. He counted my tackles, assisted tackles, and always gave me the best possible totals. Hal Wingo later became a senior editor for *People* magazine and covered our prison ministry with a big spread on several pages of that popular magazine.

I knew it wasn't just luck. God had arranged it that way. Everything was just falling my way and I knew it. I felt unusually blessed. I wasn't that good, just living in a blitz of blessings. In some ways I was still a fatherless boy on the end of the bench, on the third string.

But I was in love. My every thought was of Mavis and I was so blessed that she was equally as excited about our marriage. We met in October of 1956 and were married six months later, on the second of March, 1957. Again, God took care of us. We were "Me Too"-ing decades later. Even to this day we are amazed by our great compatibility. We are so alike and even our differences have a way of filling each other's weaknesses. She likes to follow, I like to lead. She likes to travel but also likes to build a nest at home. I like both of them. I enjoyed my 12 years of pro football, she liked it even more. She loves our children and I love them even more. (She of course, would disagree.) She loves me; I think I love her more. Again, what a great argument to have: "Who loves who more?" I felt unworthy of all these blessings. It was just grace (unmerited favor).

JT KEEPS POPPING UP

Mavis' father, Parker Knapp, taught Sunday school for teenagers in Harlingen, Texas for 30 years. JT Williams was stationed in Harlingen in the Air Force. He also taught Sunday school in the same department.

Most Sunday lunches he followed Parker home after church for a home- cooked meal. So, Mavis and her two sisters were fond of JT, and since they were three of the most beautiful girls in town, there's nothing not to like about visiting there for JT! He went on to serve as general chairman of our Tallahassee, Florida city-wide crusade 20 years later. He was a highly respected CPA and land developer. He was obviously a respected Christian leader in the Sunshine State's capital city.

When we married in March of 1957, JT was among the special invitees on Mavis' side. I remember the big church was packed; I was pleased with the beautiful ceremony, but had eyes only for my bride.

Most of my groomsmen were Baylor football players. My brother Vernon was my best man. He had been All State in high school and was a pre-season pick to make All America his senior year at Rice, but the team had a bad year and he didn't go pro. Charlie Bradshaw, another groomsman, could not be missed at the front of the church, standing 6'8", and weighing 300 pounds. He played 12 years in the NFL. Bill Anderson was our great tight end and went on to spend the rest of his life pastoring great churches in Florida and Texas. My great friend, John Preston, was also a big lineman who played on the freshman football team with us. That group of groomsmen could have suited up and been an all star football team.

Mavis' beautiful sister, Rosie, was matron of honor, and their cute 11-year-old sister, Gretchen, was also a part of the wedding party, along with my sister, Linda. It was a big event in Harlingen, with a beautiful reception that followed at the country club.

BAYLOR BEAUTY CONTEST

Every year at Baylor, 10 women are nominated for "Baylor Beauties." Mavis was one of the nominees. The judging was done in Houston by a group of actors and other celebrities. The judging for the contest was to take place the day of our wedding. Mavis explained to the committee that she was getting married that day and she wouldn't be participating in the contest.

The lady in charge called and applied pressure of every kind to get her to understand what an honor she was passing up. Mavis explained that she had turned all of the details of her marriage over to her mother. She was planning receptions, showers, luncheons, which would last for an entire week: All the dates were set! Mavis insisted that it was much too late to change anything. She sweetly apologized, but firmly informed the woman that she wouldn't be present.

"This shows disrespect and is a snub to Baylor and the Baylor Beauty contest," the woman complained. When she pleaded further, Mavis held her ground.

"I've lived for 18 years in Harlingen and am much more concerned about not hurting friends and family there, than with a four- or five-month friendship with Baylor," she said.

"My husband to be is taking me with him to Canada to play professional football," she went on. "I'll not see most of my Baylor friends again, but I will see my family and friends. My decision is final."

I even tried to talk her into it, but she just laughed. It was a waste of our time, she assured me, to discuss it any further. She couldn't care less what they would think or say about her! For the first time I was able to see a side of her that I had missed. When she makes up her mind, it is a waste of energy to argue with her.

Harlingen over Baylor, wedding over contest, she had firmly decided. "You are the only one who ever passed up appearing at a Baylor Beauty contest," the lady in charge assured Mavis. But Mavis was certain that she was right and there was no changing her. If you asked her, "What did the Baylor Beauty people think?" she would say, "I don't actually care what they think. I did the right thing!"

Mavis and I went on our one-night honeymoon to Brownsville, 20 miles away that evening. Then we flew to William Jewel College in Missouri for a Religious Emphasis Week on their small college campus. The students, about our age, teased us about our newlywed status, but we had a great time. I'm sure nothing could have messed up our honeymoon. Sure, it may have been better to slip away to a private island where no one knew us, but we had a great time anyway and we felt fulfilled serving Christ at that little school.

As an added blessing, I got to spend a lot of time with the man who would become my mentor, Fred Smith. He was also one of the speakers that week. It had only been a few months since I was introducing him to Baylor audiences. Now, I was on the program with him. From there we went on to Kansas City where we spoke in a big church on Sunday. Mavis and I were back at Baylor the next day.

SURPRISED AGAIN BY BLESSING

You may wonder why "blessing" is so pivotal. Because among other and even more important things, it means that people are freeing each other to prosper. My dad did this often as he sat on my bedside and blessed me almost nightly. Coach Stages did it, by yelling instructions to me, in the one-on-one drill, sitting beside me on the team bus, and in the weight room. In film study when he'd say things like, "Watch Bill—he had a field day." I thought he always gave me the benefit of the doubt. He even made me one of seven captains my senior year in High School! I doubt that I really deserved it.

He talked me up to college coaches who were trying to recruit me to go to their schools. I had many college scholarship offers and visited many schools. Again, I just wasn't that good. Stages built me up so much; they had to give me a break. Sooner or later the college coaches would mention something Coach Stages had said to them about me. He often said, "I think he is virtually unblockable." When college coaches used phrases like that, I knew where it came from. This kind of blessing did indeed free me to prosper. But it also made me feel a nagging unworthiness. Maybe they just felt sorry for me and thought they ought to give me a break. One thing I knew for sure, I was playing at my best, really prospering!

I challenge you to try it with your loved ones. You'll "free them to prosper!" It's easy to love your Heavenly Father, when you feel blessed by your earthly Father. In my case, it was a father substitute.

MENTOR AND FATHER SUBSTITUTE: FRED SMITH

At Baylor every year they conducted a program called Religions Emphasis Week. They brought in some of the most exciting Christian leaders to speak in chapel and at nightly rallies, and even in the classrooms. I was the chairman of the program in my senior year. I selected myself to introduce my favorite speaker, Fred Smith. He was a management consultant to many major corporations all over the world.

Fred was brilliant. He spoke 42 times during that one-week period. I know because I hosted and introduced him all over the campus to classes, rallies, chapel services, even the football team. What a rare blessing! He seldom repeated himself. The questions and answers were the best part. I took notes and learned so very much from Fred. I soon started to realize that our relationship was unique. Not exactly the relationship Coach Stages and I had shared, but not totally different.

Stages provided mentoring and blessing that was oriented toward football. Fred was mentoring me mentally and spiritually.

Both men had a certain fondness for me and me for them. Fred assured me that he didn't like to be syrupy, or overly emotional. Fred explained that he could not mentor someone he didn't like. This was his way of saying, "I'm fond of you, but don't want to get too emotional and actually come right out and say so."

He said, "Have you ever noticed that almost without exception, when a man calls he will, within the first few minutes, indicate his purpose for calling?" He wasn't comfortable saying "I just wanted to call because you are a real friend." I let it pass, simply agreeing that his observation was true. I later called him back to say that I often called him just for relationship reasons, no other purpose. He said, "Yes, but you don't count, you're family." I felt blitzed by his blessing! I was like a son. But he had, for once, actually said so. He really wasn't comfortable to formally state, "I'd like to be your substitute father." If in our exchanges he could make it clear without getting "touchy- feely" he was okay with that.

My most treasured times with Fred were late in his life. He was on kidney dialysis. He needed help getting to the dialysis center, where he had to stay for four hours getting his blood cycled through a blood cleaning process. We would often spend all four hours in excited discussion, other times he'd sleep without apology, which I encouraged. I always brought a book to read. He was a big-time reader, himself.

When his eyesight failed, I read to him and brought books on tapes for him to listen to. I bought him a book by Randy Alcorn titled *Heaven.* He loved it because the writing style was believable and down to earth. Fred felt that his lack of formal education was a blessing because he was always trying to make up for not having attended college by reading everything he could. How many college graduates stop developing their mind after graduation?

For years after I graduated from Baylor, we would share the keynote speaking duties at conferences, retreats, and other gatherings. But even after I was sharing equal billing on these speaking engagements, we always had a mentor relationship or even a father-son relationship. I treated him as my elder and superior. To this day, I consider him to be the wisest man I've ever known. I can think of many high-achieving Christian leaders who share my high esteem for Fred Smith.

MY LAST WORDS WITH FRED

The last time I saw him was in a hospital. We talked and prayed and as I was leaving, I knew I would probably not see him again until Heaven. So I turned back to say my final words to him. His huge feet were uncovered, as usual— he liked to leave them uncovered—so I grabbed his big toe and affectionately squeezed. "Fred, I know you don't like the syrupy stuff, but I must tell you, I look at you like a father. You have been my greatest human strength, and I love you!"

Tears flooded my eyes, even as I tried to stop them. I turned quickly and lunged for the door so I wouldn't really blow the top off the "syrupy scales." I knew that would make him uncomfortable.

Then I heard a grunted response from him. I turned in the doorway and choked the emotions back and said, "Sir?" He gruffly repeated, "Mutual!" He said it as if he knew I heard him, but was simply forcing him to repeat it, and he was right. We both chuckled. I recounted this final encounter with Fred at his funeral. Everyone agreed that this was an expression of his ultimate blessing. Our mutual friend, Jack Modesett, said, "That is classic Fred Smith!"

BLESSING MESSAGE IN PRISON

For years, I have spoken in prison about everyone's need for the Father's blessing. A lack of the Father's blessing is the cause of almost all violent crime. "If you want to keep your children out of prison, bless them. Tell them you love them," I say to them. Fred visited me in my office often and on one of his visits he said, "I was listening to your blessing message on my CD player coming to your office today and it was really good." I replied with a thank you, and then remembered speaking of him in the message. I described him as a man of towering wisdom, of deep spirituality, 84 years old and one who had blessed me like a second dad. I quickly asked if he knew I was speaking of him. He answered, "Sure I did." I pressed, "But I didn't mention your name." He impatiently said, "Who else do you know who has towering wisdom, is 84 years old, and blesses you?" We both broke into laughter. Fred never bragged, except to poke fun at himself.

Our office building for Champions for Life is named "Fred Smith Memorial," and there is a bust of him in the foyer, which is the first thing you see upon entering the building! Lee Roy and Tandy Mitchell helped pay for our headquarters building and agreed with me it should be named after Fred, and insisted on the bust.

LEE ROY AND TANDY MITCHELL

The Mitchells were good friends of Fred Smith. He brought Lee Roy to a men's meeting at his church, Highland Park Presbyterian, in Dallas. I was speaking there that day and we soon became involved in a share group in Tandy and Lee Roy's home. Lee Roy said he gave Tandy an unlimited budget to build the home and she exceeded it. It is the most beautiful home I've ever seen but most warm and inviting and only exceeded by the humble spirit of Lee Roy and Tandy.

Mavis loved Fred and Mary Alice (Fred's wife) and she soon grew to love Lee Roy and Tandy just as much. We enjoyed their beautiful home, but soon grew to love them as dear friends. Down-to-earth, warm, sweet, open, and all three couples were able to mesh. We called our monthly dinner meeting a "share group," not a Bible study. We often used the Bible as a departure point, but we weren't under pressure to use it, if it didn't fit. The conversation was usually about spiritual things, but sometimes we ranged far afield. The tears were always close to the surface with Mary Alice, who shared her innermost feelings freely. The group rallied around hurting ones. Sooner or later everyone, without exception, went through some hurt, certainly including me. We "wept with those who wept and rejoiced with those who rejoiced (Romans 12:15)."

We all became so close. I even privately (just the three of us) discussed with Lee Roy and Tandy his prostate surgery. I explained that I knew Lee Roy was concerned about how the surgery may affect their sex life. We prayed about there being no problems and the *Amen* was accompanied by a giggle. Tandy reported to me after surgery that Lee Roy was just fine. I always felt comfortable in talking about anything and everything with them and they were the same way with Mavis and me. It is probably better not to discuss some subjects, sex among them, but this seemed to be an exception, because of the type of surgery. We laughed together, prayed together, served Christ together in our little group and in prisons.

Shortly after we met, Tandy honestly told me she wasn't sure she knew Christ, so I called one day on my way out of town and said, "I don't feel comfortable leaving town until we've settled your spiritual questions!"

I met with Lee Roy and Tandy in Lee Roy's office and carefully led her to the assurance of her salvation. They have both served on the Champions for Life Board of Directors and I admit they are among our best friends. Fred Smith introduced us, but our friendship has continued long after his death.

CHAPTER 4

CANADA & THE NFL

A CANADIAN BLESSING

I played my first year in Canada in 1957 for the Saskatchewan Rough Riders for three reasons. First, I was legalistic and Sunday football was a no-no. Second, my line coach at Baylor had been Coach Wilson, and he had just been hired to be the line coach for Saskatchewan. Also, a lot of our players from Baylor were on this Canadian team. Stan Williams, a great tight end, had been All-American at Baylor and Larry Isabel, the Rough Rider quarterback, was also a Baylor man. Both Isabel and Williams were on the Baylor team two or three years before me. They also offered me $14,000 in Canada and only $12,000 in Detroit. $2,000 was a lot of money in those days.

I really didn't like Canadian football. Mavis and I stayed sick with colds and flu half the time. A lot of Canadian football rules were so different that it seemed like a different game. Stan Williams was a good friend on the team and my roommate, which was great. But I played poorly because of the negative atmosphere, and my own inner battles. Late in the season, they took me off the active roster for four games and I was miserable.

But I was reactivated for the last two games and played extremely well. I intercepted two passes in one game and ran them back for great yardage. In those games I was the star, making tackles and interceptions all over the field. That really made my year in Canada turn out better, because I ended the season on a high note.

But actually Canadian football was "bush league." There was only the head coach and two assistant coaches. The team was owned by a committee of townspeople and their team office was the business office of one of the committee. Their stadium only seated 15,000. But I wasn't even playing up to bush league standards, so there was no way to feel good about my first year in the pros. Still, when they pleaded with me to come back, I declined. I was certain that I wanted to play in the United States—no more second-class team for me! I was unhappy with myself. It wasn't the team's fault. It was just a mediocre experience. I expected more of my performance and needed a new start. I wasn't ready to give up my dream.

LOOKING FOR A BLESSING IN DETROIT

The next year, I switched leagues to become a member of the Detroit Lions, having been their first draft choice the year before. I rationalized working on Sunday, but I think genuinely a New Testament Christian isn't bound by "keeping Sabbath days." (Colossians 2:16: "Do not let anyone worry you by criticizing what you eat or drink, or what holy days you ought to observe, or bothering you over new moons or Sabbaths.") That was the verse I relied on to help me justify my Sunday play. I also knew that the NFL would give me a huge platform. When I played in Canada no one in the U.S. knew or cared.

The Canadians themselves weren't bush league at all. They were delightful and friendly people. I often went hunting with teammates, which was great fun: The hunting was always successful. We always killed a lot of the bountiful game. I also preached in many churches all over that part of Canada. Mavis and I were treated wonderfully by people on the team and in the town and in the churches.

But I would have never been happy until I went home to play in the NFL. I would have always wondered if I could make it in the big leagues of NFL football. At least I knew I had to give it a shot. So I signed to play with Detroit in 1958.

I was shocked and even nauseated by the Lions' totally pagan lifestyle. Perhaps it was exactly what God wanted me to experience to help me get over my legalism. I needed to face the pagan world with a sense of realism. I certainly had a baptism by fire with the Lions. If Saskatchewan was the bushes, then Detroit was the big leagues of wild living. Bobby Layne, our star quarterback, led the constant party crowd. Tobin Rote was the backup quarterback, and had led them to the Championship the year before when Layne got hurt. They traded Layne to Pittsburg mid-season, and I was glad they did. I was playing center and these two quarterbacks made life miserable for me, because they blamed me when the snap wasn't exactly like they wanted it. After Layne was traded, things were less stressful, since now there was no quarterback competition and I only had to snap the ball right for one quarterback, Tobin Rote. He was Son's old competitor at Rice, but that was never discussed. I'm sure it was a sore spot for Rote and I know it was for me, because of my loyalty to Son.

One of the Lord's first commandments is "let your light shine so that they may see your good works and be drawn (Matt 5:16)." The best translation of this passage is "attractive good works." Our Lord conflicted with the Pharisees continuously because their "good works" were unattractive to others.

If one could do the reverse of the Pharisees then he would attract people, not run them off. They were careful to pray in a public place so that everyone would see their piety. They were anxious to have the exact number of tassels on their robes to have the most outward impact. Christ pushed for internal righteousness. "Pray in your closet," He insisted.

Christ said they were like "white tombs on the outside, but full of dead men's bones on the inside." The law truly kills but the spirit makes them alive (II Corinthians 3:6). But slowly, I came to realize I would have much more acceptance and witness if I quit being so judgmental. I may not have been criticizing peoples' sins out loud, but in my own mind I was self-righteous and I'm sure they felt it.

Even Layne could be halfway friendly at times. After cussing me out for a mistake in the way I snapped the ball to him in an afternoon workout, he'd take me out to dinner to a nice restaurant that evening. But after dinner, he insisted that we go bar-hopping until the wee hours of the morning. Since I didn't drink, I was the designated driver.

When Layne was traded to Pittsburgh, I was moved to defensive end. This was my perfect chance to remind Layne of how the whole world had changed. He cussed me out so much that it was a relief to see him cuss out his offensive tackle and ignore me. We were playing an exhibition game against Pittsburgh. I had dreamed of getting an opportunity to sack Bobby Layne. I actually didn't have hate or revenge in my heart. On second thought, maybe I did, in my worst self. Mainly I wanted to show him that I was a better player than he thought. Anyway, I was super motivated. I sacked him six times in that one game.

He'd jump up, cussing the tackle that was trying unsuccessfully to block me. He was making an obvious attempt to totally ignore me. So the next time I sacked him I made it a point to hold him down long enough so that he was sure who was on top of him. He struggled to get up, but I simply tightened my grip on him and pinned him like in a wrestling match. He wanted to jump up, so he could cuss out his own tackle, but I was determined to not allow him the privilege of ignoring me. What a fun game that was! Layne was getting old and soft and I was still young and strong, so I really enjoyed putting him in his rightful place—flat on his back!

WADDY

Watson Spoelstra was a sportswriter for the *Detroit Free Press* when I went to play for the Detroit Lions. "Waddy" was what everyone called him. I met him because he covered the Lions for his paper. He came to Christ about six months before I met him. His daughter had suffered a brain aneurism and the doctors expected her to die.

He tells it this way: "I was a hard-drinking, womanizing, dedicated pagan. Not interested in God and not too much time or love for anyone but myself. But, I got down on my knees in the Catholic chapel of the hospital and begged God to let my daughter survive brain surgery and get well. I promised God if he would heal her, I'd get right with Him. She did get well, and I turned to God."

When I came to Detroit, he was a baby Christian. I helped in his spiritual growth. We met almost daily for Bible study and prayer. I was going to seminary in the off-season, so I was sharing some of my new-found knowledge with him. He was 50 at the time and I was 25, but we were close friends. We had to keep our meetings secret because my teammates might have thought I was trying to butter up the press in order to make the team, via more favorable press coverage. Actually, he bent over backwards to not favor me in his daily stories for the paper. As a first draft choice, I pretty well had the team made anyway.

Waddy needed a lot of Christian fellowship, and so did I. The Lions were a wild group of guys. He fit right in with them before his conversion. But, afterwards he didn't have anything in common with them and neither did I. We'd meet in his hotel room on road trips and in secluded places on the little private high school campus, where we headquartered for training camp. It was called Cranbrook School for Boys.

A school not just for boys, but little boys—as evidenced by the fact our players kept hitting their heads on the door closers that hung over each doorway. The trainers wrapped the door closers with foam rubber to protect the taller players, who were practically getting concussions from them. It was a very elite private school and looked more like a small college campus. We had our six-week training camp there every year.

It followed a rugged schedule of two workouts per day, with meetings at two different times during the day. We had six exhibition games and fourteen league games. Now they just have four pre-season games and sixteen league games. Training camp was tough to survive. I couldn't bring my family along and I missed them terribly. We already had one son, Billy, and Bobby came along 18 months later. Mindy followed three years after Bobby.

There were no outspoken Christians on the team that first year. So I really was glad to have Waddy as a friend, and he was eager to grow spiritually. I got along with my teammates pretty well, but did not have even one close friend on the roster. They looked at me as an outsider and didn't want me to beat out one of their veteran friends, and told me so. But, again, since I was a first draft choice the year before, they had to keep me on the team. Everyone knew I was studying for the ministry and didn't drink, smoke, or cheat on my wife. So I was not a good fit with these hell-raisers. Alex Karras was a rookie my first year in Detroit, he was a first-round draft choice. So we had two first-rounders on the defensive line.

But I was doing well on the field. During "one-on-one" drills in practice, I put my Stages moves on them and beat everyone, including their All-Pro center Charlie Ane, a big Samoan. I was also the fastest lineman.

During a live scrimmage against another NFL team, they staged a race between all the backs and a separate race for the linemen, and I won in the race of the linemen. They gave the winner $15. I thought, "What a deal!"

I was moved to several different positions and finally ended up at defensive end. George Wilson was the head coach, and he was as wild as the players. He encouraged a wild lifestyle. Wilson's rowdy Lions team had won the championship the year before, but they weren't that good my first year with the team.

I was the starting defensive right end my second year in Detroit, but never lived up to my potential in this rather hostile environment.

I preached in a lot of churches in the Detroit area, just as I did in Canada, and made many Christian friends—but none on the team. Marshall and Fran Garvey became our best friends. We went to the same church. He was an attorney and they continue to be our friends today.

But, slowly, I was making some headway with the players. I tried to fit in better without getting into their sins. But my legalism was a problem. Again, I was a Pharisee on the inside, but never openly put them down. But I'm sure they could feel my disapproval of their lifestyle. I don't blame the Lions players for my lack of acceptance on the team. I was an unattractive Pharisee. I'll have more to say about this in Chapter Nine. For now, I'll just say I was glad when they traded me to Cleveland. The Browns of that era were a classy outfit and I fit in much better, but it was primarily because I had decided not to be a Pharisee.

When I was traded to Cleveland, I decided to intensify my efforts to avoid the Detroit mistakes. Since I really couldn't change my teammates' lifestyles, I decided to work on myself. My witness was noticeably more effective. My five years in Canada and Detroit hadn't been wasted, even though at the time I felt they had. I learned a lot about how to relate to the pagan world. I needed the Canadian year to mature before going to the NFL. Detroit was a wake-up call. They were the "gas house gang." They made an art form out of being totally corrupt. Their language was profane. Their sins were blatant. They were honest about their lifestyle, but it was unapologetically Godless.

The underworld was often hanging around on the edges of the team. I was not surprised to see some of them getting one-year suspensions for a gambling connection a few years after I left Detroit.

Honestly, I had no first-hand knowledge of any gambling, and doubt that they were betting against themselves. For that matter, gambling in any way that it would hurt the game, except when they were kicked out for that year.

I admit that I would have fit in better if I had followed I Corinthians 9 and became "All things to all men"—not partaking in their sins, but not even thinking self-righteous, judgmental thoughts. Perhaps, this was the Lord's way of moving me more gradually toward prison ministry because of course, a judge isn't what convicts need. They need forgiveness and the big thing was to grow as a football player and improve my execution on the field.

LEARNING TO PLAY THE KEYS

Don Shula had been my defensive coordinator my first year at Detroit, and he coached me better than any pro coach I played for. He taught me, among other things, how to play keys. It was really quite simple.

As a right defensive end, the first key is that when I came up against the first player that could block me—the left tackle—I had to hit him with a forearm or hands shiver with arms locked at the elbows, to ward him off my body and to keep good separation. As Stages taught me, never let them touch your body between the shoulder and knees. Get off the line fast and never get tied up with the blocker.

The second key is the second player that could block me, the offensive end. Often he would be split out and was not a factor. But if he was lined up as a tight end and blocked down on you, you must ward off his block and "string it out," forcing him to the sidelines.

When you get blocked that way it's usually an end run. Expect help from your outside linebacker and defensive backs and turn the play in or string it out to the sidelines.

The third player key, the onside back, Shula taught me, could also be dealt with: "If he blocks down on you again," he said, "you must hit him hard enough to get his attention, but don't let him tie you up and fight to the outside, it's an end run, fight for outside contain. If he tried to turn you out, fight for the inside. It's an off tackle run."

The fourth key (expect the onside guard) was that, if the tackle blocks down, close down on him and get ready for the crossing on-side guard. Fight off his block and expect a back carrying the ball between the guard and tackle.

The fifth key, the one to the off-side guard, was that, on a trap play, "close down" on him. It's coming up the middle; destroy his block and tackle the back!

All five of those keys must be played in order. Tackle, tight end, on-side back, on-side guard, and off-side guard, but it must be repeated so often that it is on automatic replay. It becomes a reflex action, done without conscious thought.

That which you repeat under pressure tends to groove itself into permanence. These keys that Shula taught me I used for the rest of my football playing days. He didn't remember, I'm sure, but his instructions were even being used by me when we beat his Baltimore Colts, four years later in the World Championship game, 27-0. He was their coach that year before moving to become the head coach and have fabulous success at Miami.

Blanton Collier had an even better football mind, but couldn't take time to do individual work as much, since he was the head coach. But Collier did more individual coaching than any Head Coach I played for. He knew and taught the details of every position. He loved to teach you step by step. Again, I enjoyed my four years with the Lions, but never really lived up to my footbal potential. Shula went on to coach the Miami Dolphins to the only perfect record of any team in NFL history—seventeen straight wins!

In the off-season I went back to seminary at Southwestern Baptist in Ft. Worth, Texas. I was just finishing my fourth year at Detroit and counting my first year in Canada, I was returning to seminary to start my fifth off-season studying theology. I always enjoyed this totally different off-season work. It was graduate-level studies and challenged me to the max. We had bought a home in Ft. Worth and I enjoyed spending a lot of time with the family and going back to school. We had just moved in and registered for the spring semester when I got a call from Waddy. He told me I'd been traded to Cleveland and I was surprised they hadn't told me yet. I was pleased he called because it gave me time to think about my reaction to the coaches and press.

Within minutes of hanging up with Waddy, head coach George Wilson called to express his regrets for having to trade me. Then Coach Paul Brown called to say how pleased he was to get me in a six-man trade. Three players were traded to Cleveland and three players from Cleveland went to Detroit. The Browns traded Milt Plum, Tom Watkins, and Dave Lloyd to the Lions for Howard Cassady, Jim Ninowski, and me.

"Ever since I coached you in the Senior Bowl I've wanted to trade for you," Brown explained. It was billed as the trade of the year, but as it turned out, I was the only one of the six who was a starter after the trade. Two quarterbacks were included in the trade. Milt Plum went to Detroit and Jim Ninowski went to the Browns; both were injured and never became starters again. All six players had been starters before the trade. Injuries and other problems arose. It was the best thing that could have happened to me. Cleveland was a class team, a much better environment for me than Detroit or Saskatchewan.

I went to the Pro Bowl four times during my seven years with the Browns. That would have never happened at Detroit. More important, it gave me a chance to shape up my attitude toward non-Christian teammates and repent of my own Pharisaical attitude. I was determined to have a whole new start with the Browns.

CHAPTER 5

CLEVELAND

THE BLESSING OF THE BROWNS

In Cleveland they weren't angels, but the comparison was like daylight and darkness. Head Coach Paul Brown ran a tight ship. He wanted his players to be classy in their dress, table manners, and personal conduct. He constantly lectured us on all of those subjects. Some players griped about his demanding requirements, but to me it was a welcome relief to be on a classy team. Suits and ties for all public appearances, on the road and at home, good table manners and language on all occasions were requirements. He was 17 percent owner of the team and the team was even named after him. He exercised complete control.

Amazingly, the owner, Art Modell, fired him after my first year with the Browns. Modell complained that, "It was like firing God!" It was not a popular decision with the Brown's fans, but Blanton Collier followed Brown and won the World Championship in 1964. He coached the Browns to winning records and into the playoffs every year until he retired in 1973. He retired primarily because he had a hearing problem and he thought it hurt the team.

To measure this impact of Brown's firing in Cleveland would be comparable to what happened in Dallas years later when Jerry Jones, owner of the Dallas Cowboys, fired Tom Landry. Even with this new leadership, winning Super Bowls hasn't totally erased fan resentment for the firing of one of the most respected coaches in the history of the game. It happens.

Modell's decision followed a rather disappointing 1962 season and Paul Brown elected to stay out of football for seven years until his contract was fulfilled with Cleveland. He came back to the NFL as an owner of the Cincinnati Bengals, primarily with money he made from his seventeen percent ownership of the Browns.

Twelve years after I retired, in 1980, Brown selected my son, Billy as his fourth draft choice. Inflation was dramatic in professional atheletes and Billy was paied $80,000 as a fourth-round choice. I had made $14,000 as a first-round draft choice. Two years later his teammate from Baylor, Mark Addicks, was paid $2.4 million. (That's how fast salaries were jumping!) That's not even close to what modern salaries have done, the minimum rookie salary in 2010 is $320,000.

I often visited with Paul after my son, Billy, was on his team. We took up where we left off in my playing days. I continued to like him. He traded for me and drafted my son. What's not to like? He was a class individual. Again, Collier knew more technical football and was a major factor in the Browns' success when he was an assistant for Brown.

THE BLESSING OF A NEW START

I consciously tried to not be "holier than thou" and genuinely love my teammates and, as it says in I Corinthians 9, to make every effort to become "all things to all men," in order to win them over. Six times in that one Chapter, it repeats "to win the more." What things do you become "to win the more?" It is clearly stated in that chapter: You have to become a servant, a Jew, a man living under the law, a man without the law's protection and, of course, "all things to all men [and women]," in order to "win the more."

While playing for the Lions, I knew I had failed to adapt to my teammates, and so I had withdrawn. I avoided their parties, but I had to admit Christ actually put more life in the party by making what turned out to be the best wine (first miracle). He was a friend of the tax collectors and never threw stones at sinners. Was the wine He made better because it had less alcohol? I doubt it; everyone at the party agreed it was the best. What party-goer would like grape juice?

When I was traded to the Browns I had a new start. This time I was going to make a real effort to be as winsome as I could be, and to be a better salesman of my cause. I even made a list of my new goals. First, was to be a better player on the field. Second, was to aggressively avoid being a moral policeman, or censoring anyone's lifestyle—though not to be a partaker in activities that were against my moral convictions. Third, was to never duck witness opportunities, so I was constantly explaining my lack of interest in cleaning up my teammates' morals. (Look in Chapter 9 under "Why I Encourage Cussing" and the Tim Tebow discussion). Fourth, I wanted to start a chapel service before all games. Fifth, I swore to go along with them where possible, just to keep the door open to witness. I didn't personally drink, cuss, or cheat on my wife, like some of them. But, I didn't make a big deal of it or try to make them feel censored by me. Even when I totally disagreed with them, it wasn't necessary to say so.

I've heard people say, "The reason I'm not popular is because I'm a Christian." I have often felt like saying, "Maybe you aren't popular because of your rotten personality. Don't blame God because you are so boring!" I'm sure I wasn't a very winning personality during those years I played for the Lions and even in Canada. But I was sure I needed to change in order to be a more attractive Christian, and the trade helped me to make that change. It gave me a new start.

I tried everything to be a team player. I often started snowball fights after practice. I constantly looked for ways to stay involved with my teammates, even juvenile pranks. I went to their parties, and had Bible studies and dinners at our house, which Mavis cooked. I spoke up and asked questions in team meetings. Politely argued with coaches about strategy on the field and always entered discussions about our team and any other discussions where I knew enough to get involved.

I made friends with black players and tried to bridge racial barriers. I started chapel services for our team and encouraged other Christians, like Raymond Berry and Don Shinnick, to start chapel services on the Baltimore Colts and other NFL teams. As far as I know, the Browns chapel service was the first in the NFL and the Colts was the second. Baseball followed football and had chapel services, some of which were led by Waddy, my friend from the Lions days.

My wife bought me a red suit and I wore it to a team dinner. Coming down on the elevator after the dinner Jim Brown had a talk with me. He said, "We, the black players on the team, just had a meeting and we voted you the most improved dresser on the team!

When you came to the Browns you were the worst dresser ever, but that red suit convinced us you were easily the most improved!" This became a joke on the team. The white guys and the black guys kidded me about my award, "The Most Improved Dresser."

I had tried to be the best, truest, most Christ-like, non-Pharisaical, loving and attractive Christian I could be. When a teammate snubbed me, I decided not to let it pass without comment. I asked him what I might have done to offend him. I could tell I'd done the right thing. He was totally embarrassed and at first denied the snub, and I reminded him of what he had done. He agreed he had treated me with a lack of respect. He apologized and we were better friends after I directly confronted him.

I refused to withdraw, as I had in Detroit. My success and that of the team on the field helped. My first year in Cleveland, I was the team leader at sacking the quarterback and continued to hold that leadership for six years in a row. Playing well and helping your team win is the most important way of getting respect on any team.

There is no doubt that the true Christian must adapt to the lifestyle of the non- Christians. The question is how much to move toward their lifestyle. At least far enough to have Paul warn against "falling away" (2 Thessalonians 2:3).

MONTE CLARK

My teammate and close friend, Monte Clark, rented a house across the street from us in suburban Cleveland. Early in our relationship, Monte, in a hard-fought game, was kicked in the scrotum and it swelled to basketball size. On a daily basis our team doctor would insert a large needle and drain two or three tape cans of fluid from the swollen scrotum. He would climb up on a training table and the procedure began. Monte complained about this process on the way to practice that morning, my curiosity got the best of me so I slipped into the training room to watch. Monte yelled in pain as the fluid was sucked out with a large needle. At first, I thought I was the only one watching, but soon I looked around to see at least half the team cringing in sympathy and a few nervous chuckles could be heard even though Monte's groaning drowned them out. Most everybody felt really sorry for Monte, as he was suffering great embarrassment and even greater pain! To add to his torture, he had two or three boils on the back of his neck, which had to be lanced on several occasions.

Several players attended a weekly dinner and Bible study held at our home or in the home across the street shared by Monte and his wife, Charlotte. Mavis was cooking Mexican food, which all the Texas, Oklahoma, and other southern players loved. Back then, there were no Mexican food restaurants in Cleveland, or anywhere in the north. So Mavis' Mexican food was a meal everyone looked forward to. Frank Parker, our big teammate from Oklahoma, wasn't a great Christian, but he never missed Bible study when Mavis made her Mexican dishes.

But the funniest moment in any of those evenings came when Mavis innocently inquired, "Monte, how are your boils?" With her Southern accent, it sounded like she said, "How are your balls?" The players were uproariously laughing. The women hadn't been told about Monte's major problem and really didn't know what was so funny. Mavis knew she'd made a real mistake so she repeated, "You know, the boils on your neck," pointing to her neck. But it was too late to correct and by then, the laughter was so loud that no one could hear what she was saying any way. That was the best Bible study we ever had—plenty of laughter, warm friendship, and great Mexican food.

My two best friends with the Browns were Christians and participated in the chapel service and Bible study. Monte Clark and Paul Wiggin were really great guys who both became NFL head coaches shortly after their playing days. They were most encouraging with their suggestions about football and life! Both continued coaching for decades in the NFL as head coaches or assistants.

Our friendship continued after football. I officiated at Monte's funeral in California. Many coaches and players attended the funeral. They were friends that he played with throughout his life, or had coached. Mavis and I still stay in touch with Charlotte, Monte's wife.

Paul Wiggin is probably the best-liked former coach or player. Everyone looks up to Paul, he is so positive, gracious, genuine, and intelligent. He was Head Coach at Kansas City for three years, and at his alma mater, Stanford, for several years. He was also an assistant coach, and later an administrator, for the Minnesota Vikings for 25 years. He continues as a consultant on staff with the Vikings even now.

Jim Shofner and Jim Ray Smith were also great Christians on our team and continue to be close friends, and live in the Dallas area. Jim Ray is retired from the real estate business and served on our Champions for Life Board of Directors and Jim Shofner served in the prison ministry as a platform guest. He was an assistant coach in the NFL for 40 years and Head Coach where he graduated many years ago at TCU.

THE BLESSINGS OF FAITH AND FAMILY

Again, for my first six years in the NFL I studied at Seminary during off-seasons, earning my degree in 1963. During training camp I got special permission to rent an apartment near Hiram, Ohio, close to the Browns training camp. Then, during the season we were only gone one night for each road trip. We played 14 league games and six exhibition games, so we were away from home only 10 nights, which gave me time to be a good father to my two sons and daughter, and, of course, a good husband to Mavis. It also gave me an opportunity to maintain some important relationships.

My Baylor buddy Charlie Bradshaw and I continued our friendship for 12 years in the NFL and on throughout the rest of our lives. He played for Pittsburgh and Detroit and I played for Detroit and Cleveland. We celebrated Thanksgiving one year in Cleveland at Frank and Joan Ryan's home. They owned a huge country home, and it needed to be plenty big for our expanding families. At the time, we each had two or three children.

Dr. Frank Ryan, holder of a PhD in mathematics, had a scientific mind. He was our quarterback for the Browns when we won the World Championship in 1964. Frank was an agnostic, and that challenged both Charlie and me intellectually, but it was interesting that he invited two Christian couples to his home for Thanksgiving. I'm certain he was searching. We spent a couple of days together with no arguments—amazing! Charlie, Frank, and I were engaged in hot debate on many occasions. But, this was Thanksgiving and we were in the last stages of a tough season, so we wanted to keep the atmosphere peaceful. It was a pleasant Thanksgiving with family and friends.

At the 40th reunion of our World Championship team, we were together privately and Ryan asked if our debates about spiritual things had weakened my faith. I assured him to the contrary— they had only sharpened and defined my faith more clearly. The scripture says, "Be ready always to give an answer for the faith (1 Peter 3:15)." I was impressed that he had worried about hurting me. It showed he had a good heart, as well as a good mind. Maybe he had just mellowed through the years and wanted to be more compatible, and I'm sure I have. When we were teammates 40 years before, I was studying apologetics (arguments for the validity of the faith) at Seminary and I tried all the arguments I was learning on him, which resulted in heated debates. I think I was able to win some of the debates because I had the arguments well organized. But I think I wasn't successful because I was too aggressive. You can win the argument and lose the person.

Charlie became a most successful attorney in North Dallas, but he had many rough edges when he first came to Baylor. He made no apology for his many mistakes in grammar, or for his anger at girl-friends for eating all their food, nor for his love for debate on any subject. I was glad I didn't have to debate him about some mistakes I made in speaking at his funeral. Fortunately, his children were too polite so I got by with saying what I liked at the funeral. He died too young, but he lived a great life.

My greatest joy will be to sit on some park bench in heaven and talk to him for a few thousand years. The conversation would go something like this: "You sure had the dean frustrated when you explained in detail about how to make a hood. But, you saved my life with Mavis on that first date at the cafeteria when you admitted how you expected a girl to leave part of her food for you! I know I took too long, preaching at your funeral, but I sure appreciated you not interrupting me before

I was through. I knew you were watching closely (Hebrews 12:1)! You have to admit there were some good things said about you that day by all of those teammates and lawyers." He would say, "Lawyers are a mix, some phony, some surprising, but the players were really good!"

That would be my side of the conversation. I'm sure he will go on at length and be most entertaining. Hebrews 12:1 says that all the saints in heaven watch us here on earth, but in Luke 16 Christ himself tells a story about a rich man and a poor man dying. If I were telling the story, I would have finished when they died, but their dying doesn't end the story. He continues the story by following them to heaven and hell. But, He rejects the rich man's request to be brought back from hell to warn his brothers. Christ's summary was, "If they won't listen to Moses and the prophet then one risen from the dead won't do any good!"

THE BLESSINGS OF KNOWLEDGE

Our 1964 team won the World Championship, two years before the Super Bowl began, and they were a class bunch. Our quarterback was Dr. Frank Ryan. Paul Wiggin was a graduate of Stanford with a masters degree. My degree from seminary was equal to a master's degree. I spent six off-seasons of graduate-level study to earn it. I was a full-time student the entire off-season, and could never let up in my studies, in order to pass the requirements. I am so pleased I did the hard work necessary because it prepared me well for my ministry in city wide and in prisons. The diversity of the ministry God called me to demanded a solid seminary education.

There are some, Fred Smith for example, who don't need a graduate education, but I must admit that I benefited from every study hour I spent in the seminary. Looking back I see that period when I would spend half my year in seminary studies and other half in the NFL made for a well-rounded, maturing experience.

My theology could never get too other-worldly, because it was always bumping head-on with brutal reality. Sometimes Seminary Hill can be too "other-worldly," and that does no earthly good. I always came back to Seminary eager to study and learn. I really never got burned out, the way some of the year-round students would. These students proceed all the way through college, got their undergraduate degree then headed right on through Seminary for their masters or doctorates without ever experiencing front-line ministry experience. One may think I stretched my education out too much, taking six years to do three years of study. But I really don't think it took too long, because my theology was tried and proven in the most practical way— in daily "head butting," physically and mentally, in the NFL, and then back in Seminary for some real mental and spiritual head butting. Again, it was just another blessing of God.

THE BLESSING OF A WITNESS

I had to make it a rule that I wouldn't accept speaking engagements during the week. I needed to study. In order to prepare for graduate level studies, it was a must! I did agree to weekend engagements, but never through the week. But I got a call from a particularly determined young minister, who insisted I speak in Ruston, Louisiana, at a youth rally on a Wednesday evening on a date a year and a half in the future. In a weak moment I agreed to the 300-mile trip. It was a 600-mile round trip and I had a big test the next day. I got home at 3 a.m. and had to stay up the rest of the night studying.

I wrote the entire experience off in my mind as a total failure. Mavis asked how things went. I answered, "I'll never agree to a school night engagement again! There was a good crowd, but only one little 'cotton headed' boy trusted Christ. It's just not worth it, while I'm trying to go to Seminary."

Ten years later I started receiving articles from all over the country about Terry Bradshaw, the No. 1 choice in the NFL draft. The articles told how Bradshaw was asked what the single most important factor in his upbringing had been. He replied, "When I was 11 years old, I went to hear a pro football player speak and I made a Christian commitment."

"Who was that player?" they questioned.

He said, "Bill Glass. He played for the Browns when they were World Champions in 1964."

Terry Bradshaw was the little "cotton headed" boy in Ruston at the youth rally! I had written it off as a wasted evening! Only heaven will show us what we did of value in this life; until then, as the Bible says, "We see through a glass darkly (1 Corinthians 13:12)."

THE BLESSINGS OF VICTORY

Many of our teammates had graduate degrees because it was a good way to spend the off-season. Whatever job you could get for six months during the off-season wouldn't pay enough to be more valuable than a graduate degree.

After I completed my seminary degree, I was able to spend my off-seasons as I wished. I spent most days with my children. We built forts

96

made of barricade fencing and dug caves. The caves were simply holes dug four or five feet deep and covered with wood and tar paper and dirt grown over with grass. There was a short tunnel coming up through the floor of the fort and a long tunnel led to the big room. It was lit by candles. We spent hours digging and roofing and building. Other hours were spent in the main room and tunnels fighting imaginary enemies with sling shots and BB guns.

The first three years after Seminary, I preached at many different venues, and took the family with me, except when our children's school schedules interfered. I always hurried right back from speaking engagements to be with the family when they couldn't go. All summer they traveled with me; during training camp I spent time with them every day at the apartment. But I still had to be back in the dorm at Hiram College in time for our 11 p.m. curfew.

I was anxious to spend as much time with my growing children as possible. After 12 years in football I started to feel more and more that it was time to retire from the game and follow my greater calling in ministry. But I was torn because playing in the NFL was a great platform from which to witness. We averaged 80,000 in home attendance in Cleveland and constant TV coverage. In many ways, the NFL was more important then, than it is now. Except for player pay, it was really a better game.

One of the most treasured trophies from my NFL career was a letter I got from my friend and teammate, Paul Wiggin. He is more respected than anyone else I know among players and coaches. He spent decades as an assistant coach and director of pro player personnel with the Vikings.

Wiggin was a great defensive end, going to Pro Bowls twice and playing for 11 years with the Browns. He was the left defensive end and I played right defensive end. He retired as a player in 1967 and became an NFL coach. Paul spent seven years as an assistant with the San Francisco 49ers and two years as the New Orleans Saints defensive coordinator. He was Head Coach of the Kansas City Chiefs for three years (1975-1977), and then went back to his alma mater, Stanford University for four years as head coach (1980-1983). Since then he has been an assistant coach and administrator for the Minnesota Vikings until now. Terry Pluto (Pulitzer Prize-winning sportswriter with the *Cleveland Plain Dealer*), in the best Browns book ever written, *Browns Town* 1964, quotes Paul as saying:

> *"If you were to ask me what was the greatest feeling in my life, it was winning that championship," Wiggin said 30 years later. "I don't wear jewelry. I don't even wear my wedding ring. But for years, I wore that championship ring. My wife asked me why, and I tried to tell her that for one moment in my life, nothing has ever meant as much to me as that championship. It only lasted a short time, but to have that feeling about being the best in the world…"*

Wiggin paused, searching for the right words.

> *"As I walked out of the Stadium that day, there was a telephone pole," Wiggin recalled. "I wanted to climb up that pole and just yell to the whole city of Cleveland that I was part of the best football team in the world—and I know that the city would have understood what I was talking about. We had a group of guys from Georgia, California—you name it. White guys, black guys, it didn't matter. Nothing mattered except on that one day, we came together*

and did something very special. I have spent the rest of my life in pro football trying to duplicate that feeling, and I never have."

I couldn't agree more, that World Championship was certainly the highlight of my years in pro ball. Paul was a great leader and if he had suggested we both climb that pole, I would have been right with him, even if we would have looked foolish yelling from the top of it!

Paul was normally much too sophisticated for anyone to even imagine him doing such a thing. But, that day I wouldn't expect him, or any of us, to react in a normal sort of way.

I admit that, "If what you did in the past still seems big, that means you probably haven't done much lately." Obviously, I consider the ministry I led to be of more ultimate importance, but I also agree with Paul: *That was a pole-climbing day!*

This letter came 40 years after I retired from the Browns:

May 2007

Bill:

Shortly after you were enshrined in the Brown's "Hall of Legends," you called me and asked about your sack totals and I have finally got a validated study of the Brown's sack numbers. Bill, I had the privilege of playing with you from '62 through the '67 seasons. During that stretch you had 74.5 sacks (21.5 more than I had) and for those six seasons you averaged just a fraction under 12.5 sacks per season. I have chosen football for my life's work just as you chose the ministry and I know about sacks and for whatever it is worth -these are Hall of Fame numbers! If you could have started your career (I believe the same as mine) with the Browns in 1957 and had the same average for those to add on with the 74.5, your total would have been 137! Also, after we both retired, there was a big "QB Preservation" trend and one of the earlier rules was called "in the grasp," which made sacks much easier, giving a span of years in which some of the modern "big names" got the advantage in padding their numbers. They also had the advantage of playing two more games (16 as opposed to 14) to add to their totals. What is even more amazing is that in this modern realm, getting a sack brings on a dance that you would associate with curing cancer—when we sacked the quarterback we treated it like it was something we were paid to do and like we had done it before! Bill, give my best to the beautiful Mavis and I hope all is well with you two as well as your family. Very little time passes without wonderful memories of those Cleveland times— and about teammates like you that made those times so special.

Sincerely,

Paul

I'm certain I played better at Cleveland, partly because of Paul's encouragement! Early in my first season with the Browns, Paul said, "You may not even know it, but the last guy to wear number 80 was Lenny Ford, and he always led the team in sacks. Now you are wearing that number and it looks like you'll also be our sack leader." I thought, "How unselfish, because Paul had that title before I came to the team!"

I am aware that Paul is a great friend and is probably giving my career a very generous benefit of the doubt, but I am including his letter simply because he is a respected teammate and coach. I probably got all of the recognition that I deserved and more. I have felt uncomfortable writing this book, writing parts of it that say too much about myself, but I guess an autobiography is by definition self-centered. Paul included the following statistics on sacks with his letter.

Browns' Sack Totals, 1962-1968

1962
Bill Glass – 13 ½

Paul Wiggin – 8

Robert Gain – 7

Floyd Peters – 5

James Houston – 4

Michael Lucci – 3

Frank Parker – 2

Vince Costello – 1 ½

Samual Tidmore – 1 ½

Galen Fiss – ½

1963
Bill Glass – 9 ½

Paul Wiggin – 8

James Houston – 3 ½

Robert Gain – 3

Frank Parker – 2

Galen Fiss – 1

Bernie Parrish – 1

1964

Bill Glass – 10 ½

Paul Wiggin – 8 ½

Richard Modzelewski – 5 ½

James Kanicki – 3

Frank Parker – 2

Galen Fiss – 1

Stan Sczurek – ½

1965

Bill Glass – 15 ½

Paul Wiggin – 9

Richard Modzeleski – 7 ½

Walter Johnson – 2 ½

James Kanicki – 2 ½

Sidney Williams – 2

James Houston – 2

Dale Lindsey – 1

1966

Bill Glass – 14

Paul Wiggin – 10

James Kanicki – 4 ½

Walter Johnson – 3 ½

James Houston – 2 ½

Frank Parker – 2

John Brewer – 1

Vince Costello – ½

1967

Bill Glass – 11 ½

Paul Wiggin – 9 ½

Walter Johnson – 8 ½

John Brewer – 6 ½

James Kanicki – 4 ½

James Houston – 3

Frank Parker – 1

Dale Lindsey – ½

1968

James Kanicki – 10

Ron Snidow – 5 ½

Walter Johnson – 3

Jack Gregory – 2 ½

Marvin Upshaw – 1 ½

Dale Lindsey – 1

Bill Glass – 1*

John Garlington – ½

Bill Sabatino – ½

*(injured most of the season)

I guess I'm more proud of the fact that my boys still remember that day with great joy. We beat Baltimore 27-0, when everyone had picked them to win by a wide margin. The boys were waiting at a point where the tunnel went beneath the end zone bleachers and they jumped aboard my shoulders and rode triumphantly into our dressing room. They were riding double, one on each shoulder. They were actually in the dressing room of the World Champions and sharing in the sheer joy that followed that most victorious day. Few non-players were allowed in the dressing room. After the game, we all attended a player's party and dinner that Mavis and our three children enjoyed and the celebration continued until after midnight and for years thereafter. That 1964 Championship is the last time any Cleveland team won a professional title.

THE PASSING OF ONE GLORY TO THE NEXT

Moses went up on Mt. Sinai and met with God and came back with the Ten Commandments. His face glowed with the glory of God. But in II Corinthians 3:13, Paul reminds us that it was a fading glory. So, Moses covered his face with a veil so the people wouldn't see the fading glory. In 1964 we won the World Championship! The very next year pro football instituted the Super Bowl. Over 40 Super Bowls have come and gone since then and the glory of that pole-climbing day has faded.

When Roman generals came home from victory in battle in the glory days of the Roman Empire, shortly before and after the first century, there was always a huge parade. Marching in the parade were the general's cavalry, foot soldiers, conquered slaves, booty, bands, and then came the victorious general in a golden chariot in full parade battle dress, preceded by trumpeters bugling his triumphant return. But there was also a slave who stood behind the general in his chariot who repeated over and over again, "All glory is fading!" There is one glory that doesn't fade, the glory that becomes ever greater from "glory unto glory (II Corinthians 3:18)." Not the letter of the Law that Moses brought down from Sinai, but the spirit of Life in Christ (II Corinthians 3:6).

I have a whole room full of trophies and memorabilia from my college and pro career. But I'm sure that, when I die, you can pick them up cheap in a garage sale. It's like a fading crown of leaves that will go back to dust, no different from our decaying bodies after death. It's as the slave repeated, "All glory is fading," except the glory that comes from the Lord (II Corinthians 3:6).

FIGHTING TO COME BACK

My last year with the Browns was 1968. Wiggin was gone, having retired as a player and taken a coaching position with San Francisco. Jim Brown had retired in 1966 and the team was changing. We were in the playoffs every year and still a power in the NFL but never went to the Super Bowl. When I got to training camp that last year before I retired from the game, they told me that Jack Gregory, who was 10 years younger than I, would be the starter. He had been a backup for Wiggin and me for the previous two years. But Dick Modeleski, my former defensive line teammate, was now our new defensive line coach. He explained the decision this way: "As long as you're the starter, Gregory will never develop." I was really angry. I had been the sack leader for my first six years with the Browns, and gone to the Pro Bowl four times. Sure, I was 33, but I had never been hurt and was as strong as ever.

I met with Collier and Modeleski and told them I wished they had told me before I made the long trip from Texas with my family. I wouldn't agree to quietly sit on the bench and play a backup role. I was going home, I would just retire, or maybe they would trade me. But they obviously didn't want me to retire, because they would be left with two untried defensive ends, with Wiggin and me both gone.

They appealed to my team spirit: "You can't leave the team in a bind, and you could back up both defensive ends and probably get to play a lot." But I was determined not to settle for a backup position.

So, I had a brainstorm and suggested, "We've got six pre-season games. Let Gregory start all six and play for the first half and let me play the entire second half. Then closely grade both of us and whoever does the best becomes the starter for the regular season."

I had a good exhibition season and our comparable grades were clearly in my favor for the first five games, but we were preparing for the final game of preaseason against the Buffalo Bills in their stadium. As we prepared for our final exhibition game, in Buffalo against the Bills, the coaches were not talking to me about who was winning the competition for the starting job. I was determined to have a great game in Buffalo.

Jack Gregory played well in the first half but got no sacks. I was praying and busting a gut that I would dominate in the game. It turned out to be a thrilling afternoon. I got six sacks in that last half. Jack Kemp, who later made a name in politics, was their quarterback. I was so very thankful to God. Everyone was congratulating me on a great game, but still there was no clear word from the coaches. I wanted to hear them say, "You are our starter; you won the contest!" But they didn't say anything except, "Great second half."

The first clear-cut indication that I had won the job came from Art Modell, our owner. He obviously knew about the competition. He met me just before I got on the team bus to return to the airport, for our chartered flight back to Cleveland. He gave me a big hug and a clear statement, "I've talked to the coaches and they say you are our starting right defensive end for the season. What a great game, six sacks in one half!" I thanked God all the way to the airport and to this day remember this as an outstanding victory! I truly felt blitzed by blessing!

CHAPTER 6

CITY-WIDE

BILLY GRAHAM AND MY CALLING

Billy Graham's role in my calling was a real surprise, but how God brought it into a reality was even more obviously God's providence. I had already felt called to some form of Christian service. That's why I studied at Seminary for those first six off-seasons. I completed those studies in the off-season of 1963. The next football season was 1964, when we won the World Championship. I'm sure this was perfectly timed by God. Graham invited me because winning the championship brought a lot of attention to my Christian witness. Every time I sacked the quarterback or even made a tackle they would mention that I was studying at Seminary for a ministry in Christian service.

It was to be his first nationally televised crusade in Denver, and he asked that I give my testimony. I continued to share in other Graham crusades. I never really felt called to pastor. I felt God had blessed me with a gift of evangelism.

Grady Wilson, one of his staff members and a close friend to Graham, said, "You know, Billy thinks you are called to city-wide crusades." I replied, "I know, but it frightens me and how can I know if it is truly God's will? I'm convinced that it is important to be absolutely certain of God's calling." Grady replied, "What Billy says is that there are four ways to know God's will." He explained them to me like this:

- First, an open door! You certainly have that with the fame and opportunities the championship is bringing.

- Second, you need a reasonable preparedness. You have just graduated from seminary and you have preached hundreds of times already.

- Third, you need the counsel of Godly people. I think Billy is a Godly man, don't you?

- Fourth, an inner impression! Spurgeon says you must have a "Divine Oughtness!" You must say with Paul "Woe is me, if I don't preach the gospel." This is the one that only you can know.

Billy must have really been after me because, when I had one hour of uninterrupted time with him, he opened up to me. He started by saying, "You know, I'd give anything if I was as strong as you are. I can't take some medicines because I'm allergic to them. So, I just have to suffer through whatever illness I catch. I really don't know how long I can keep it up; the pace I'm going is killing me!" He obviously thought he wasn't going to live a long life. Little did he realize, he would live into his nineties.

"Grady told me he had told you about my four-way test to know God's will," he continued. "But, even if I can survive 50 more years there is still a need for other men like you, who are called of God. It's my opinion that you should seek God's will concerning your calling. I've heard you give your testimony several times at our crusades and I am certain that God has given you the gift of the evangelist."

I replied, "I'm praying about it." The subject was dropped, but I continued to give my testimony for him in city-wides and have enjoyed his continued blessing.

A BLESSING FROM BILLY GRAHAM

Billy Graham's personal blessing meant so very much to me. Not only the time in Denver, but on a number of other occasions where I gave my testimony in his crusades. On several occasions, he sent our ministry (written from first to last in his own hand) a gift. It was always the same amount: $1,000. Even recently I got this email:

"Word has reached Mr. Graham of Bill's surgery today. I am writing to extend on behalf of Mr. Graham and our association our prayers and encouragement to Mr. Glass and to all of you at Champions for Life. We are praying Philippians 4:19 specifically today and in the days to follow. When you are able, please give Mr. Graham's greetings and grateful appreciation to Mr. Glass."

But back to the time I was able to have quality time with him in Greenville, South Carolina. He was in a city-wide in an auditorium that seated 21,000. They had two services each evening at 6 and 8 p.m. Between the two services we had an hour break while the first crowd left and the second crowd came in. I asked if he'd like to have some time alone. He said, "No, I'd just like to talk." And so we did, for at least an hour. He repeated what he had said before: "I can see that God has given you a great gift of evangelism and you should pray about conducting city-wides like me."

I had not considered it until his encouragement. But to think that the greatest evangelist since Paul was led to suggest that I should follow in his footsteps! I was trembling with the blessing of this man, the No. 1 Christian leader in the world. I had so looked up to him ever since my own conversion.

We conducted a city-wide in Asheville, North Carolina a few years earlier and Graham bought a full-page ad in the paper endorsing the effort. It helped! To have the blessing of Graham appeared to me as invaluable, but in God's economy, maybe a letter of blessing from an ex-con would have been just as valid. Only God knows! But He does tend to make the last first!

The late, great Paul Meyers coined a new word when he called himself an "inverted paranoid." A paranoid has it that the whole world is out to get him. An "inverted paranoid" sees the whole world reversed; everyone is out to help him. Actually, some balance is usually correct. Only God is truly out to help in all ways and is unlimited in his ability to do so. The object of this book is to say, you can probably see why I would get a slant towards thinking "they are all out to help me." Maybe it's because I genuinely feel I need all the help I can get from God and man. But it also was obvious that there are constant reminders of God's supernatural intervention, when you genuinely feel blitzed by blessing!

OFF-SEASON PRO, ON-SEASON EVANGELIST

By 1966, I had been blessed to build a team. In the football off-season I began to conduct city-wide crusades. We were following Graham's pattern in cities like Tallahassee, Memphis, Indianapolis and Evansville, Indiana. I knew it was in God's will. The last three years I played for the Browns, 1966 through 1969, I kept it up. City-wides January through June and football July through December, or through January, when we were in the playoffs (1966-1969); what a platform the NFL was providing!

During the season, I started NFL chapel services prior to every game and over half of my teammates attended each week, some of them found the Lord for the first time or made a new commitment.

Our big linebacker and team captain was Jim Houston. After one of the chapel services I noticed he was staring out of the window in deep thought. I asked if he had enjoyed the chapel speaker. He said, "He was great, but it made me realize I need to make certain that I know Christ myself." I led him through the plan of salvation and he prayed to receive Christ. To this day I see him often on trips to Cleveland. He was a platform speaker in our first Weekend of Champions in the prison in Marion, Ohio.

I felt so blessed to be fruitful, both in and out of football. Huge crowds gathered in football stadiums in great interdenominational and interracial city-wide crusades!

A couple of years ago, Gordon Heffern called to tell me a story I had never heard. A friend of his from the city of Youngstown, in eastern Ohio, called to tell of his son, who was a part of a little gang of five teens who had been going bad. They were involved in alcohol, pot, and petty crimes. The father was alarmed and decided to bring them to a city-wide crusade I was conducting in Canton, Ohio, in the football stadium. It had only been a couple of years since I retired from the Browns. The boys were fans and were anxious to come see what was happening in Canton, the football capital of Ohio and home of the NFL Hall of Fame. They were curious to see this ex-Brown and hear what he had to say.

All five boys came and all of them trusted Christ that evening. "And now," Heffern reported, "all five are in some form of Christian ministry." I called the president of Dakota Wesleyan College in Mitchell, South Dakota. I wanted to get the "rest of the story" concerning these five young men. I never even met the young men the night they came to the Canton crusade or since. They were dealt with in the counseling room and returned with their group to Youngstown.

But as the city-wide ministry grew and matured, football became less and less important. I was again blessed to have my college education and now my seminary education all paid for by football. But the real blessing was seeing God work through our team. I was genuinely called out to lead evangelically. I honestly often felt that I was just a spectator on the sidelines watching what God was doing. I never felt worthy of His calling me to such an awesome ministry. Colossians 2:6 "…the walk in Christ is through faith, grace is the right attitude, never merit always grace."

As I said before, I got special permission to bring my family. No one brought their family to training camp, but I insisted and the Browns agreed. By now, my sons, Billy and Bobby, were eight and six and my daughter, Mindy, was three. Mavis was young and beautiful, physically and spiritually. She was perfectly adapted to our life on the road in football and ministry.

THE BLESSING OF FISHING IN BIGGER PONDS

As I've said, I was anxious to spend as much time with my growing children as possible. After 12 years in football I started to feel more and more that it was time to retire from the game and follow my greater calling in ministry But, I was torn because playing in the NFL was a great platform from which to witness.

I was getting more invitations to preach or speak in churches or at banquets or conventions than I could possibly have time for. So when I would get several invitations from one area, I'd write them with a city-wide proposal.

"Why don't we meet in a football stadium with cooperation from all the churches?" I'd ask. You know you increase the size of your fishing pond, if you include all denominations and all races. Include everyone, the scripture says, "Uttermost part of the world." That says it all: We must be all inclusive! "If I were a Christian I sure wouldn't be a Baptist," I heard someone say. Or maybe they have prejudice against some other denomination or race, but if we meet in a stadium and all are involved that takes away those objections. Interracial and interdenominational was always our objective— any way to have a bigger fishing pond.

In 1966, Liberal, Kansas was the first to agree. We were in the high school stadium for a week. The crowds came, the response was excellent. Ron Patty (Church of God) led the music. His wife Carolyn played the piano; his young daughter did solos. She later became one of the best-known Christian singers in the United States, Sandi Patty.

Bob Andersen was our instrumentalist, a musician who could play the organ and piano at the same time, what talent! The piano was placed at a right angle to the organ and he played them both, one hand on each. It was really quite amazing. It was like having an entire band on stage! He also ran the sound system, which was saying a lot because our venues were so widely diverse— football stadiums, fairgrounds, gyms, auditoriums, wherever! It was a challenge, which Bob seemed to handle well. On many occasions we used black ministers of music and platform guests. We were determined to be more inclusive.

Perhaps the best thing about the Liberal, Kansas crusade was meeting Jim Wickwar. He was staying in our motel for the week and came to the crusade a couple of nights. He was a tire salesman and traveled and sold tires in many parts of Kansas. Everywhere he went he talked about the Liberal city-wide crusade. He invited us to his hometown of Colby, Kansas. We were there for an entire week and had a fantastic crusade, where people from miles around found the Lord. We ultimately got invited to Hutchinson, Salina, Dodge City, Topeka, Joplin, Springfield, and several other cities in Kansas and surrounding states. God used that tire salesman to spread the word about our ministry.

We ended up receiving phone calls and inquiries from cities all over Kansas. The caller would almost always sound like this: "I was talking to a tire salesman and he told me about what God did in Liberal and Colby." I said, "Jim Wickwar told the truth, again!" Wickwar never was on staff, but continues, to this day, to serve God through our ministry. One excited and committed person can be used by God in fantastic ways!

We conducted more city-wides in northwestern Ohio than anywhere. It was the perfect place. I'd played in Detroit and Cleveland for 11 years so I was well known because of football. Also, it was a highly churched area, and no one denomination was so strong that they didn't need the other churches. There were still a lot of people who didn't know the Lord, so evangelism was definitely needed. In many cities, then and now, there were mega-churches that didn't cooperate in city-wide efforts. They were, and are "too big to fail!" They were not so cooperative with their smaller brother and sister churches!

Anyway, we went back to Findlay three times. That was where Jack and Judy Ridge and Gene Kandel led the local committee. It is amazing what lay leaders like these can do to open doors and lead in a local community. You are miles ahead in your efforts when you have this type of leadership.

We eventually served in city-wide crusades in every county in that corner of the state at least once and in many cities we returned for city-wides often. We also went to most of the schools with the athletes speaking with Champions for Today (our school assembly programs) and prisons with our Weekends of Champions. More about those later.

Another great leader of local committees was Steve Luce. Steve was for many years our board chairman and even served as CEO for nine months. We met when I conducted a city-wide crusade in Perry, Georgia. He slowly became involved in our Weekends of Champions also. He and Mary Lu, his wife, still serve on our board. He came out of a family of dedicated Christians who also ran Blue Bird Bus Company. They built school busses until they sold the company. They were the biggest in the United States! I wrote him for his permission to put this in the book and inquired about his family, and he said they are all involved in Christian service—what a family! But it is something you can expect since they've been doing it for generations. They've handed down the blessings of service to others. Unfortunately, convicts pass down a life of crime to their children and grandchildren. Parents who don't think that lifestyle is good or bad will see it show up in the future in their descendants.

In the off-season after my last year as a player, we were conducting a city-wide in Topeka, Kansas. I called a press conference to announce my retirement from professional football. Again, God arranged it to get the maximum, an all-out blitz of blessing, and the headlines were much the same all over the country.

What are the odds that Joe Namath would choose to retire the same day that I did? Namath and his teammates had won the third Super Bowl in an awesome game after he predicted the victory. Headlines everywhere read "NAMATH RETIRES TO OPEN A BAR IN NEW YORK; GLASS RETIRES TO FOLLOW HIS MENTOR BILLY GRAHAM INTO CITY-WIDE CRUSADES." Our lives were such obvious opposites and most sportswriters just had to comment on the great contrast, which of course was a boost to our ministry. Again, what are the odds that Namath would choose to retire the same day that I did? God's providence blitzed again! Since Namath was the quarterback for the first AFL team to win the Super Bowl, his retirement was bigger news than mine. He was modeling panty hose in magazines, and even on TV! He even bragged about his many sexual partners. I was preaching in city-wides and soon even prisons. No one asked me to model panty hose. I was far too big and ugly. It might have been funny, now that I think about it, but it sure wouldn't have helped sales.

As I said, I was always seeking to build a bigger audience. We found that if the city-wide crusade was interdenominational it made for a much more diverse turnout. I was Baptist by background, but never wanted that label. We wanted to be genuinely interdenominational. We were always using secular venues. Football stadiums or auditoriums were best. Meeting in any church would cut out too many people. We always insisted on being interracial, both in the audience and in the leadership.

Also, my message had to be well chosen so as not to offend anyone's theology unnecessarily. Not too Calvinistic, Pre-millennial, Eternal Security, Tongues, or Anti-tongues, in other words, I always avoided the controversial subjects. There is so much that most evangelicals agree on, it is not necessary to offend.

In 1970, Pastor G.L. Johnson called to ask me to preach a revival at his People's Church in Fresno, California. He was Assembly of God, but we've never had a disagreement in 50 years of very close friendship and partnering in ministry! I suggested a city-wide, he agreed and most churches of all denominations cooperated. We went to their public auditorium and the place was jammed nightly, crowds of 7,000 plus. Then we were invited to the south, to Visalia, population 50,000. We gathered in the football stadium with about the same size crowds. They gave $30,000 to us for our prison ministry work in 1973.

We returned to Visalia about once every decade for three different city-wides. Lory Bennetts and his wife, Nancy, hosted 17 banquets in their beautiful backyard. Several hundred of our backers gathered in preparation for city-wides or prison weekends! Lory served on our board and backed us in our ministry in California and nationwide.

Bill Pruitt, one of our best coordinators for the Weekend of Champions, was also from Visalia. His church wouldn't cooperate because they called their church the Independent, Pre-millennial, Fundamental, Separated, Baptist Church. So, naturally, they wouldn't cooperate with this interdenominational crusade, but Pruitt came and also followed us into our Weekends of Champions. But he could not get anyone from his church to join him to serve in prisons. He tried to persuade others to join us in the Weekend of Champions prison ministry, without success, for five years. Finally, he got one man from his church to come to a Weekend of Champions. That guy went home and recruited five friends from his church to join us on a Weekend of Champions. Within a brief length of time the number grew to 31 from that church and even the pastor joined us on a Weekend of Champions.

Bill Pruitt discovered that 30 out of the 31 who had served in the prison with us were able to lead someone to Christ back in Visalia, within the first month after the Weekend of Champions. The pastor said, "I've been teaching soul winning for 20 years in this church and only have, possibly, five people who would actually actively win the lost. But after one Weekend of Champions, 30 people led someone to Christ!" When we came back to Visalia, conducting a city-wide, that church was one of the most actively involved!

In our last city-wide in Visalia I met a number of people who had found Christ in the early 1970s in the stadium crusade. Their children had been converted in the early '80s and their grandchildren in the early '90s. To meet three generations of converts was a great encouragement!

After our first Weekend of Champions in Marion, Ohio, our next trip was to California, the Tehachapi prison, outside Bakersfield. The

Weekend of Champions prison ministry became the mission arm of the city-wide ministry. My great friends in the Bakersfield city-wide, Ed Green and his wife Sue, picked up the tab for the entire Weekend of Champions at Tehachapi prison. Most of the inmates turned out for the programs. Jerry Enomoto was the warden and he soon became commissioner of the entire California prison system. He insisted that all the state's prisons invite us for a Weekend of Champions.

During my pro career the biggest salary I ever made was $35,000 per year. I probably was one of the least successful players financially among my teammates during those championship years and afterward. The only extra money I ever made was from a ranch I bought in West Texas near Hamilton. I sold it 15 years later and doubled my money. But I never made any money, to speak of, from our city-wides or our prison ministry, just enough to live on. Billy Graham was a great example of real integrity by the way he handled money. I followed his example. Too many Christian leaders have lost their impact because of poor stewardship of funds.

RANCH LIFE

My father-in-law and his wife, Parker and Mavis Knapp, left us some money in their will, so I have been off-salary from the ministry for the last nine years. We did "pass the hat" once in prison and never got the hat back—joke, ha!

I put some of my football money into the down payment for the ranch. We loved the ranch. During the school year, we lived in Waco for the first three years after I quit pro ball. Then we moved to Duncanville, a southern suburb of Dallas. I had to be closer to the Dallas airport so I could travel.

We moved to the ranch every summer when the kids were out of school for the three months of their summer vacation, and traveled to the city-wides and prison from there. We all loved the ranch. We had a simple small ranch house, but a large pond on our 1,172-acre spread. There was a year-round flowing creek running through the middle of the ranch and huge pecan trees to offer shade. We kept 50 to 75 head of cattle grazing at all times, and sold their calves.

I was a city boy, raised in town, and knew nothing about ranching. My dad died when I was 14 and was seriously ill for the last two years of his life, so he taught me nothing about mechanics or even the most simple handyman skills. I had to learn everything about ranching by hiring cowboys. They would teach the boys and me all the skills necessary: fence building, hay baling, windmill repair, working the cattle, castrating calves, spraying for flies, feeding, and many other things. Our boys learned how to work and it was a valuable lesson, which they have put to good use their whole lives. Even Mindy, my daughter, got in on those hard work-type experiences. Being a girl, she never really had to get down and dirty like the boys, who were four and six years older, but she and her mother helped in a lot of ways: cooking, washing clothes, driving the truck and cattle trailer to the sale barn. Meanwhile the boys and I would finish working a second load for the upcoming sale at the cattle auction in Hamilton.

At night we would usually go hunting, spotlighting for varmints, which included jackrabbits, cottontail rabbits, coons, and armadillos, red foxes, and bobcats. We came back with twenty to forty varmints per night. I'd drive and the boys would stand up in the back of our truck and prop on the top of the cab and fire away. Mindy always came along, but stayed inside the truck with me. She thought her brothers were "murdering the Easter Bunny" and often insisted they not shoot cottontail rabbits, because they were Easter Bunnies. The boys agreed to shoot only jackrabbits—they had long ears and ate grass that the cattle needed. We had read that three jackrabbits ate as much as a cow, so they needed to be thinned out. The boys did a lot of thinning. Mindy would usually fall asleep in my lap before we got back to the house, and I would carry her to bed. She has recently admitted faking sleep to get me to carry her to bed. The boys and I would finish off the homemade ice cream that Mavis always made for supper.

On hot days, after working a six-hour morning shift, they would go swimming in our pond. I rolled the boys out of bed at 6 a.m. to avoid the heat, which was terrible on the summer afternoons. The pond had a large pier we'd built and a trolley, which started high above our manmade dam on top of a huge telephone post we had sunk deep in the ground. The cable continued to the opposite bank where it was secured to a tree. The cable was strong, but the stick, which was attached to the trolley wheel, would get muddy and slick. Several young friends visiting the ranch with our children broke arms and legs falling from the trolley, but they loved riding it. They flew through the air at great speed, sliding down the cable on the trolley, hanging on for dear life. When they fell in the water it was great fun, but occasionally they fell over dry ground and were injured. When we sold the ranch, Hamilton Hospital went out of business. While we owned the ranch, we kept them busy!

Some days, when the boys got older, they'd drive the 10 miles to Hamilton and play golf at the country club. Again, I insisted that they get up at 6 a.m. before it got too hot and work until noon. Their reward was a trip to the golf course and they earned a small hourly wage. We had many friends and family visit us at the ranch. Son and Marilyn, my brother and his wife, and their children, my mother, and my sister Linda and her husband Mike and their family, came often. Sam Bender, our first Prison Director and great friend, visited on one occasion, but Bender never returned to the ranch, partly because his son Tommy broke both of his arms being thrown from a horse. But they enjoyed their visit, even with both of Tommy's arms in a cast!

Jim Houston, my friend and teammate from Cleveland, visited with his whole family. All the kids and even their parents enjoyed it because there was so much to do: horseback riding, swimming, trolley riding, hay baling, brush pile burning (we had huge, unwanted piles of brush dozed into enormous stacks), making homemade ice cream, cattle feeding, bird hunting, varmint hunting, fishing, and cattle working. The work on a ranch is never finished! We were fortunate to have had no snake bites. We actually saw many rattle snakes when we burned the giant piles of brush. They would race from the piles to avoid burning and we chopped at them with axes. It was all such great fun. It was so totally different than football, city-wides, or city life.

I know you'll probably never try to raise first-calf heifers. I certainly never had any reason to do so, until I bought the ranch. Again, I was a city boy; I never even visited ranches except on some very rare occasions. I sure didn't know anything about cow-calf operations.

I had just retired from the Cleveland Browns. It was 1969.

The heifers were some of the first we'd ever had, and they had an extremely hard time having their first calves. One of the heifers had a calf leg hanging out of her. The calf was obviously dead. We tied a rope to the leg and Billy, Bobby, and I pulled with all our might, without success. Then we attached the rope to our pickup and only succeeded in dragging the poor momma cow several hundred feet across the ranch. I knew the dead calf must come out! So I backed up in the truck, getting all the slack the rope would allow. I gunned the truck as fast as possible, causing one abrupt jerk and sure enough, out popped the calf! The mother laid there unable to get up, bellowing and bleeding. We all felt sorry for her. Mindy and Mavis cringed in sympathy. Billy was fourteen and weighed 240 pounds and Bobby was twelve and weighed 120 pounds. Bobby commented dryly, "Now we know how Mother felt when she had Billy!" We've laughed about that for years.

Amazingly, the heifer lived and had many calves after that with no problems. I soon learned that a calf must be pulled at a forty-five degree angle and not straight out, as we were attempting to do.

Anyway, the ranch was a great place to work and play. The cowboys and ranch owners around Hamilton got a real kick out of the Glass family. We were such novices about ranching and forever asking dumb questions. Their reactions to us were classic. One tobacco-spitting cowboy at the cattle auction barn was looking at our family with a sharp eye; seeing my two huge sons and looking at my 275 pound frame and little Mavis at 110. He drawled, "You sure do put the size on 'em," which was what they would say to sell a big, expensive bull to mate with a small, inexpensive mother cow. I replied, "But thankfully they have their mother's looks." He nodded in agreement.

By the way, they asked a lot of dumb questions about football also. I tried to be as friendly as possible, because answers to my dumb questions made a lot of difference to my ranching success. Many ranching friends offered to help us, either for free or cheap, and I needed all the help I could get.

I even conducted a city-wide crusade in the football stadium in Hamilton. The audience was filled with Christian friends like Tom and Annette Joseph and others we'd met at the cattle auction barn, at the ranch helping us, in church, at a few social events we'd attended, or at the Spotted Horse Café, a great eating place in town.

Again God worked. They came to see this ex-pro-footballer who was also the worst rancher in the county, or many of our special guests, and ended up getting right with the Lord. No matter where we held them, the city-wides were blessed of God.

There came a time at the turn of the century when city-wides were no longer as effective. The last really great one we conducted was the one in Marshall, Missouri, during the 9/11 crisis. People were turning to God by the hundreds. (That's one reason prison ministry is so powerful; everyone in prison has experienced a "perfect storm" of problems.) People in crisis are more responsive to God! On September 11, 2001, we were attacked by the terrorists and everything changed. The nation was shaken to the core.

Our problem during the city-wide in Marshall, Missouri involved the venue. We were using the high school football stadium as the venue, but the stadium had a prior commitment for Wednesday evening, meaning we would get started Sunday, Monday, Tuesday, then have to pick up and move all the way across town on Wednesday breaking the momentum right in the middle.

All of the churches in town had cooperated and all was going well those first three evenings, but I dreaded the move to the college football stadium for the Wednesday evening service. The only advantage was that it was a bigger stadium, but I feared, that too, would be a negative since there was no way it would be full. A small crowd in a big stadium is always a downer!

September 11 changed everything. It happened Tuesday morning. All day people were glued to the television watching the planes plow into the buildings. People were upset and frightened. And when we moved to the college campus stadium that evening, we didn't know what to expect. I arrived early for the service and prayed with the platform team and sat on the stage while the choir was finishing its practice. It was amazing to see students from the college streaming down the hill out of dorms, joining the President and faculty of the school in the service. There were many townsfolk coming from all directions and even people from the surrounding cities. By 7:15 the stadium was packed and people were sitting on the football field, itself. Thousands were joining the choir, singing hymns of the faith.

We started the service at 7:15 p.m. rather than waiting for the normal 7:30 start, because the place was so packed and people were anxious to worship. Everyone seemed to be in shock, what was going to happen to our world? How was 9/11 going to change things? I preached my message on "How to Win When the Roof Caves In" and it was a good choice for the message. People indeed felt like the roof had caved in on them, as it did on Job's family in the Bible. There were hundreds of decisions among the students and local people. When I gave the invitation they started moving to the front and to the counseling area. Hundreds came to Christ that evening.

We moved back to the high school stadium for the rest of the week and I knew that it was God who engineered the move to the college that night. The college students kept coming the rest of the week and people joined in the services from many area towns. The high school stadium was also packed the rest of the week. People were much more responsive than usual. It may have been "foxhole faith" but God did a mighty work through Sunday evening when we concluded the crusade. The attacks on 9/11 did cause many people to turn to God. The whole nation was in crisis and it was indeed, causing even 9/11 to "work together for good (Romans 8:28)."

But clearly, the Weekend of Champions was growing to take the place of our city-wides.

CHAPTER 7

WEEKEND OF CHAMPIONS

SURPRISED BY A FATHER'S BLESSING

When I started to work in prisons, I saw a great difference in those poor souls who were so very injured by the abuse, absence, and neglect of their fathers. It caused me to conclude that crime was the result of bad fathering. I always challenge inmates to bless their kids. Eighty percent of inmates' children end up in prison themselves, so I say, "If you don't want your children to go to prison, bless them!" But those of us who have never been involved in crime need to bless our children also. Not just to keep them out of prison, but to "free them to prosper."

Gordon Heffern served on the board of directors for our city-wide ministry, but he was also on the board of a non-profit ministry that secured jobs for ex-cons. Over a five-year period they were able to secure over 5,000 jobs for ex-cons. In that era, the 1960s, they actually thought that a job was the most important step to rehabilitating an ex-con. But they did a survey and discovered very few success stories. It became obvious to all concerned that a job wasn't the answer. So, Heffern put the full-court press on me to work in prisons. These people needed moral and spiritual development in order to help them live a good life in the outside world. A job wasn't the real answer.

I was turned off by my only prison visit prior to that time in my life. I'd visited once with the Fellowship of Christian Athletes in Pendleton Prison in Indianapolis, Indiana. What a hell hole! "It was a needy ministry, but not for me," I reasoned.

Heffern was not the type to give up. He kept pressuring me about prison ministry. I finally agreed and took a team of the toughest sports figures that I could find: Jim Houston, our All-Pro Browns linebacker, Paul Anderson, Olympic champion weightlifter, Bobby Richardson, New York Yankee baseball star, Mike Crain, judo and karate champion, and Cliff Ray, a giant basketball player. I figured we could fight our way out if need be.

I was frightened, not of the inmates, but of not having the ability to meet their needs. The inmates responded well to the sports stars when talking about sports and even listened to their testimonies. Forty inmates trusted Christ after the first program. They were dealt with one-on-one by our teammates, a handful of laymen trained in our city-wide crusades.

Later that evening, we went back to our nearby motel to have a nice meal and to share stories about the Friday afternoon program, and then to make plans for a big Saturday. Everyone was elated. It had gone so beautifully. I was relieved; no hostages, no injuries, no bad confrontations. The inmates were so appreciative of our Weekend of Champions. No one had ever, to that point in prison history, mixed in the yard with free-world people. We had lunch with them in their chow hall and had free access to the inmates all day.

WARDEN PERRINI

Pete Perrini had played for the Browns a few years earlier and was by then the prison warden. I had only been retired from the Browns a couple of years. I really didn't know what amazing concessions he was allowing us. Again, we were allowed free access to all parts of the prison and thus, close contact with the inmates. I said, "Let's make friends even if we can't make converts."

Warden Perrini was happy with the Weekend of Champions, but the sports stars and teammates were even more excited. I was happy: Now at least Heffern would stay off my back about prisons. What I hadn't counted on was the grapevine. There is a grapevine within, but also between, prisons. Other prison leaders in different states were asking, "Why not our state?" Inmates were saying, "Why not come to Texas, Oklahoma, or California with this super interesting program?" Governors would call and ask us to come with our Weekend of Champions to every prison in their state.

Often, prisoners don't have strong relationships with people on the outside. Family problems are just another symptom of the plague that leads to a life of crime. In order to have a friend, you have to be friendly. In order to have family members who care about you, you have to know how to be a member of a family. Too many inmates just float through life, never cultivating any solid relationships. Often, they learned these mistaken ways from their parents or lack of parents, but most especially from the lack of a good father.

Consider the thoughts of this inmate, who wrote this article for a prison newsletter:

"We need heroes. We need someone to look up to. We need someone who has accomplished something to give us the courage to believe in the invisible, to feel the intangible. Our fathers went out for coffee and came back with cocaine. Their hands will not tuck us in because their feet are shackled to the prison floors. Mother is out of milk and brother has just joined a gang. Moving vans have just moved Mommy away from Daddy. Together, we see them no more. The whole country has fallen into a trash can like a comic book whose story lines are out of date."

This reminds me of an inmate at Fort Leavenworth, Kansas who challenged me. I had just delivered my message, "The Blessing." This young man cross-examined me. He was handsome, articulate, sharp, and had a quick wit. His eyes stared at me hard, and I thought he was going to attack me. Instead, those hate-filled eyes brimmed with tears.

"Bill, you love your grandson, right?" he asked.

I nodded in agreement.

"I love my kid too," he said, and he showed me a picture. The boy was seven years old, very cute and it was obvious the father was proud of him.

"Bill, I came in the house one day and caught my stepfather sexually molesting my little boy," he said. "He was only three years old. It made me so mad, I ran outside to get my shotgun to kill my stepfather, but I couldn't find a shell. I was looking all over the house for ammunition, and in the meantime, my stepfather jumped into his pickup truck and took off. He knew I was trying to kill him. I had just gotten out of the Army. I was a demolition expert. So I built a bomb and blew him up."

"I assume it killed him," I questioned.

"Blew him into a thousand pieces," he said.

We were quiet for a moment.

"I guess I deserve prison," he said. "But 35 years, straight time? I mean, what would you have done in my place?"

"I would have been upset," I said.

"But would you have killed him?" he persisted.

"I would have felt like it," I admitted.

"Well, I felt like it and I did it," he said. "But where do I go from here? I have 30 more years of straight time left. Do you think it is fair?"

I agreed that 35 years without possibility of parole seemed like a stiff sentence, given the circumstances. I knew he had to have been enraged! His spur-of-the-moment attempt at shooting the stepfather was understandable, but I was sure the reason for the long sentence was the cold, calculated building of the bomb, the obviously premeditated murder.

But I sensed there was more to this story.

"Were you molested as a child?" I asked.

"How did you know?" he questioned.

"Just a guess," I said.

But it wasn't hard to figure out. Having been abused, it was natural that he'd be enraged by seeing his stepfather attack his 3 year old son. It dredged up all the long buried feelings of rage and hurt from his own abuse.

FAMILY DISASTERS

Most inmates come from families that are disaster zones. Alcohol and drug problems are common. Divorced or single-parent mothers are the norm. There is a series of "stepfathers" who are nothing more than some guy Mom brought in off the street. These men often abuse their children, and it happens generation after generation. The sins of the father (and/or stepfather) are passed down to the children.

Prison is such a culture shock, and not just to family men, but to guys who joined the gang for protection. That longing for a family is often part of what leads them to crime, because the gang demands criminal acts, as the initiation fee for membership. This gang leader tells the new recruit, "No one can crack a safe as well as you. No one is better behind the wheel of the getaway car than you." These guys are so hungry for any positive reinforcement, they'll do anything to get it, even if it means to rob or kill. Soon, they love their fellow gang members, and believe they are loved in return.

Then they go to prison and guess what happens? No one visits, not the family, not the friends, and certainly not the gang. Very few prisoners get visits, and that's probably part of the reason they're in jail in the first place. No one cared about them.

One prisoner told me, "You should have been here last week. I had this great visit."

He talked about his wife bringing along their kids. They had a picnic lunch. The sun was bright and warm, but not hot. The sky was blue. The ham sandwiches were great. The ice tea hit the right spot. The kids were happy, and they all played together.

Frankly, all the detail was more than I wanted to hear, but he rambled on and on about his great visit! His friend came up to me later and asked, "Was he telling you about the visit from his wife?"

I said he was.

"He hasn't had a visit in ten years," said the fellow inmate.

I was stunned, because the story was told to me in such vivid detail.

"Why would he lie to me like that?" I asked.

"Well, to him, it's real," said the inmate. "When he doesn't have a visit, he just goes to that fantasy and lives there for a while."

This letter from a prisoner named Dana gives a real glimpse into life behind bars:

"Quite a few of the Bill Glass counselors came through our block today. One had done time and had several family members die during his incarceration. He did receive permission to be at his sister's bedside during her last hours. She told him if he wanted to see her again, he would have to meet her in Heaven. He also explained how his mother was worried to death over him. Mr. Glass, I did all I could to keep from crying as the guy told his story. It hit me head on. It has me so emotional, as I write this; it's tough to even get it all down. I have been disowned by my own family because of my thieving ways, over and over."

This is so common: Men and women in jail, knowing that they have no family waiting for them when they are released.

One of the keys to rehabilitation is re-establishing connections with family. I visited a prison in Jefferson City, Missouri, where they built what they called a Hospitality House. It was a motel for families who visited their relatives in prison. Remember, just because you are imprisoned in Missouri or Texas, it doesn't mean that's where you live. It just means you were arrested in that state. In Jefferson City, families come not just from all over Missouri, but from several other states. This motel-like facility gives them a place to stay.

You can say, "Who cares?"

But remember, nearly all of the inmates are getting out within five years, most within three years. In addition to accepting Christ as their savior, they need a place to live once they are released. It is best if they can go home to their families. It is good for them and good for their wives and kids. It makes them more likely to want to live a straight life and stay out of prison.

"When you are released, if you don't have a family or friend waiting to take you home, they hand you $50, or whatever is in your account, and a bus ticket to your home town or the place of your arrest," said Jim Lang, who was our prison director at the time. "Not far from some of those prisons are the worst bars. The guys take that $50 (some states a little more), head straight for the bar, and drink it up. It's a recipe for disaster. They either get in a fight or end up committing a robbery for more money. It's all too common for a guy to be released on a Friday, and end up right back in the same prison by Monday."

That's why these guys need some sort of family structure. But research has shown only 10 percent of all inmates receive regular visits. Most inmates are lucky to receive one visit a year.

HOSPITALITY HOUSE BLESSINGS

The need for a hospitality house in Texas is greater because the state is so large. If the inmate's family lives in El Paso and he is incarcerated in Huntsville, that's an 800-mile trip. We heard of a mother who finally scraped enough money together to make the 24-hour bus trip, but had to sleep under the bridge. She didn't have enough money for a motel and food. In the hospitality house, it is free!

When he was incarcerated in Florida, Jack Murphy decided to make visits special; not just for himself, but for all of the inmates. After visiting hours were over, they could see out of the unit windows into the yard, where the families were leaving.

One day, Murphy yelled to his wife, "I LOVE YOU!"

She stared up at him

"I LOVE YOU!" he screamed louder.

"I LOVE YOU, TOO!" she yelled back.

Murphy told the convict next to him, "Tell your wife you love her."

"Here?" he asked.

"Where else?" asked Murphy.

"In front of all these guys?" he asked.

"Do you love her?" Murphy asked.

The guy nodded.

"Then tell her," Murphy demanded.

The guy mumbled, "I love you."

"SO SHE CAN HEAR IT!" yelled Murphy.

The guy yelled, "I LOVE YOU!"

Soon, all the guys were yelling, "I LOVE YOU!"

And all the wives and kids were screaming, "I LOVE YOU, TOO!"

That became a tradition in that prison. A little thing like that brought the wives and inmate/husbands closer. It was the public profession of love that made a huge difference.

In Huntsville, Texas, I told a group about the inmate's fantasy visit. I told them about the impact that actual visits had on the lives of men such as Jack Murphy. I said we needed to build a Hospitality House, similar to the one in Jefferson City. Well, we made it happen. The Retired Builders of the Baptist General Convention of Texas volunteered time, 300 strong, and built the whole thing in one day! It was my idea and I served as board chairman for ten years, but the whole project was a team effort. It originally had beds for 27 people; currently it can hold 55. Now, there are Hospitality Houses all over the country patterned after the one we built with Texas Baptist. Crime is a family problem, reaching the family is a large part of an inmate making it in the outside world.

(I borrowed this story from a book by me and Terry Pluto called *Crime: Our Second Vietnam*, pages 86-91.)

LAUNCHING WEEKENDS OF CHAMPIONS

By 1966, I had put together a pretty good team for the city-wides, but we had no staff, no nothing, to play the same role for the Weekends of Champions in 1972 when those started. We struggled through sharing city-wide staff and volunteers to patch together a Weekend of Champions in prison. Little did I know the Weekend of Champions would ultimately be our most important ministry.

Then up stepped two of my best friends–JT Williams, whom I had first encountered at my wedding, and my brother-in-law, Pete Redmon (he had married Rosy, Mavis' equally beautiful sister). They said they would be glad to do all the follow-up and advance work for the Weekend of Champions. They were very successful in their own businesses and had a staff to assist them. Most mailings went out of their offices. They traveled from coast to coast to do advance work for the Weekend of Champions in California, Florida, Texas, Oklahoma, Wisconsin and many other states. They made all the arrangements with prison officials, teammates, and platform guests. They even paid their own way—flying, driving, and staying in motels. They admitted to me that at least half their time was spent on the Weekend of Champions. But their businesses thrived in spite of them becoming half-time CEOs, or maybe because of their professional abilities, plus God's intervention.

We were getting more invitations than we could handle. So we decided to serve in more than one prison per weekend. First we tried three at once, then five, then 10, and finally as many as 20 different prisons on one Weekend of Champions. We simply rotated the platform guest from prison to prison, and of course the teammates stayed in one prison all weekend.

JT and Pete are organizational geniuses. We continue to this day to follow their pattern. They learned to talk prison officials into making many concessions to reach the inmates more effectively. We recruited thousands of teammates to share with the inmates one on one. Some 38,000 different teammates have joined us for at least one Weekend of Champions, but some have served with us hundreds of times. We discovered that the number of decisions were in direct proportion to the number of teammates!

We used the city-wides to promote more teammates and all surplus funds from the city-wides went to the prisons. Many city-wides really got excited about prisons and sent donations of $15,000 or even $30,000 to our prison ministry. It was like the prisons became the mission arm of the city-wides.

For five years, Pete and JT continued to carry the organizational part of the Weekend of Champions. But they finally got tired; it was just too much. We hired a full-time prison director, but Pete and JT gave us a running start in every way. I'm forever grateful for the super organization they put in motion. They built a list of do's and dont's for teammates that hasn't changed even after 40 years. They also constructed an agenda for conducting Weekend of Champions in multiple prisons. They organized drivers' schedules, airport pickups, and all kinds of other S.O.P. for a well-functioning Weekend of Champions. Even now, we continue to follow their leadership. Most important, we developed a local group of volunteers who became the leaders of what we called the local ownership team. It was much like our city-wide local teams.

THE BLESSINGS OF EXPERIENCE

It is the obvious blessing of God that we were able to benefit from the expertise of two top C.E.O.'s at a perfect time in their lives, so they could donate so much of their time and expenses.

And to think, all this was totally new! In the city-wides, Billy Graham's work provided our pattern, but in the prisons, everything was totally new. How do you run a program in the yard? Well, if you advertise it as a sports clinic instead of a church service, you increase the crowd greatly! How do we really talk the inmates' language? We added ex-cons to our platform-speaker schedule. But equally important was our choice of other platform guests. It is fine to be extremely spiritual as long as they are perfectly natural! A preachy, holy tone never works. They have to be able to talk about the inmates' interests, their needs, and to be able to confess their own weaknesses and tell their own stories, but not in a boring way. Jack Murphy served 21 years in prison. He was the original "cat burglar" and jewel thief. He is the most articulate ex-con I've ever heard. He is so brilliant that he can hold any audience spellbound! He has served on our staff for 20 years. So much for the many people who say, "You can't change the leopard's spots, or once a con, always a con." Criminals can and do change especially those who follow closely with the Lord.

It was Murph's idea to bring bikers with us. We discovered that prisoners love motorcycles. When we storm through the front gate with 50 motorcycles, it creates a lot of excitement. It awakens the whole prison.

Tino Wallenda became a regular on our platform with his spectacular tightrope show. When he stands on his head on the wire high above the prison yard, it always makes headlines in newspapers—

whether in Capetown, South Africa, Recife, Brazil, Lima, Peru, or Huntsville, Texas. The Weekend of Champions is even more effective in other countries than in the United States because it is so totally unique. They provide virtually no outside programs in other countries. This was also true in the United States before we started back in 1972. No one had ever brought programs to the yard and with free world teammates. Christian services had been confined to the chapel. We were determined to make an event which drew all inmates.

The athletes were to remain the big draw, with Roger Staubach, Tom Landry, Mean Joe Green, Reggie White, Mike Singletary, even Michael Jordan and many others appearing with us. The basketball show is at its best with Tanya Crevier, astonishing us all with her amazing ball-handling show. She is always a favorite of everyone. But again, most important is the teammate/counselor, who does the one-on-one witness work after each program.

Mean Joe Green was our next-door neighbor when I had just retired from the Browns. At that time, he was a Pro Bowl star for the Steelers. He was just starting his NFL career. He and his wife had three children: two boys, Major and Delon, and one girl, JoQuel. They all grew up together!

Billy, my eldest son, was drafted by the Cincinnati Bengals. Paul Brown was the owner, and he had traded for me and known Billy as a child. Forrest Gregg was their head coach and we had played against each other, he for the Green Bay Packers and me for the Cleveland Browns, during our 12-year professional careers. We were on a Pro Bowl team together, so I knew him well.

We became good friends with the Greens; we even had Major and Delon, ages 11 and 9 at the time, staying with us when their Dad's team went to the Super Bowl. One evening at dinner Major said to Delon, "Should we tell them?"

We questioned, "Tell us what?"

"We're going to be on national television Sunday."

I asked, "Are you going to say anything?"

"Yes," they responded, "We're going to say, my Daddy is 'Mean Joe Green,' but he's not so mean!"

When it actually aired that Sunday in a half-time segment, we were glued to the TV and sure enough watched Major deliver the "he's not so mean" line. Major laughed and questioned us, "See what I told you?"

My son, Billy, came across many opponents during his rookie exhibition season that he knew personally. His team opened against Tampa Bay, whose offensive coordinator was Bill Nelson—our quarterback during my last few years in Cleveland. After the game Billy reminisced with Nelson and they walked off the field in friendly conversation. The next week they played Pittsburgh. After that game, Mean Joe Green greeted Billy like an old friend, or a neighbor boy grown up.

The next week they played Cleveland, and since only a dozen years had elapsed between my last season and his first, there was at least one player still on the team from when I played. That was Don Cockcroft, the Browns' kicker. Several coaches, team doctors, trainers, and other front-office people were still on the sidelines to greet Billy after the game. They embraced him with open arms as a player's son grown up. The veteran Bengals noticed this and chided him because he seemed to know their opponents better than his own teammates. He grew up in an NFL locker room during the glory years of the Browns. At least his happiest memories were being lucky enough to get to be in the dressing room after every game and going with me to practice on Saturdays and exploring the tunnels, towers, and even the roof of the old Cleveland stadium. It was huge and an antique even then, seating 80,000 people.

The very next year Mean Joe Green retired, ending his 13-year career. Joe said, "I decided it was time to 'hang 'em up.' Since the neighbor kid next door had now grown up and was blocking on me, I realized I was getting too old. I had four Super Bowl rings, and not much left to prove."

I asked Joe to go with us on a Weekend of Champions. He agreed to go with us to Parchman Prison in Mississippi. He seemed to have no fear until we entered the "Sally Port." The first gate opened electronically and we were searched inside and out. Mirrors mounted on poles were passed under the van to be sure there was nothing hidden beneath the vehicle. Finally, the second gate was opened, giving us entrance to this maximum-security prison unit.

Green was visibly shaken as the second gate closed behind us. But when we were escorted into a gym filled with inmates, he was even more nervous! It reminded me of his son's statement: "My Daddy is 'Mean Joe Green,' but he's not so mean." He sure looked anything but mean when faced with these inmates.

But he soon warmed to the task. He became more confident and shouted, "You know, I've been looking around and I have noticed most of you aren't very big. I know you think you are tough guys, but as I look at you carefully, I don't think you are as tough as you think. In fact, I've seen no one that I don't think I could whip!

"When I first came into the NFL I thought I was tough also, but I discovered that I wasn't so tough. A lot of guys could deck me. There will always be someone who can beat you up. So don't get into the fighting game. I haven't seen anyone I'm afraid of, but I'm sure sooner or later someone would come along who could take me, so I don't want to challenge anyone!"

You could hear a pen drop in that prison gym. They hung on his every word!

But not every great star had a great experience. For example, in 1982, I called Dean Smith, coach of the North Carolina Tar Heels, who were then current national champions. We were going to be in eight prison units in the area. I had only met him once but he couldn't have been more cordial. After congratulating him on his championship title, I told him exactly how we conducted a Weekend of Champions. I explained, "I'd like to get one of your name players to serve as a platform guest over the weekend." He apologized that the real stars on his team were already committed for other appearances that weekend. But, he said, "We have one guy that isn't a big name nationally, but he is well known here in North Carolina. The inmates would know his name, because he was the guy who hit the game-winning basket at the buzzer in the National Championship game. Everyone in North Carolina leaped to their feet to breathlessly watch the winning shot. I agreed reluctantly to take him with us. He put on basketball clinics in six of the eight prison units where we worked. It turned out that they did know him and were thrilled to see him up close. Great crowds gathered in all of his clinics. He challenged them to one on one games and talked and answered questions. He even talked sincerely of his faith.

But the thing that I most remember was a real heart-stopper. We had another performer named Mike Crain; he was a judo and karate champion. He was talented but at times got a little wild with his show. He would take a huge, razor-sharp sword and blindfold himself while pacing back and forth. Then he placed a large watermelon on an inmate's belly. In one dramatic chop he would cut the watermelon in half. He seemed to always succeed, even with all the drama of martial arts—the huffing, puffing, and yelling.

Then to my horror an inmate yelled that he wanted to see the basketball player hold the watermelon. I was about to stop the yelling and make a brief Christian testimony, then rush him to another prison unit. But, before I could grab the microphone and stop the chanting, he had already positioned himself on the bench with the watermelon balanced on his stomach. Crain was circling his victim with his blindfold already in place and the sword flashing in the sun. There was one breathtaking moment and the sword came swiftly down and through the melon. I was greatly relieved that Michael Jordan had survived unharmed. But I remained very alarmed at seeing the melon still not cut totally through. So, Crain made two or three more chopping motions and the watermelon fell to the ground on both sides of the bench.

We were soon back in the car on our way to another unit when I asked, "Michael, I noticed that he cut your sweatpants on that last chop." Jordan assured me, "But he didn't cut me!" I pleaded, "Please just look and see for sure!" He reluctantly lowered his pants enough to see a small cut and a lot of blood. I was really worried but as it turned out a couple of almost unnecessary stitches closed the wound. The sword was so sharp that he claimed he didn't even feel the cut. But, we never talked Michael Jordan into serving with us again. He wasn't afraid of the inmates but that sword was too much.

KEEP AND POST THE SCORE

There are those who would say it is dangerous to keep and post the score, because it may embarrass or be unfair to someone. I've noticed that people who are opposed to keeping score are those who don't have a very good record. When I played with the Cleveland Browns we had a losing year in 1962 and the head coach, Paul Brown, was fired. His first assistant, Coach Blanton Collier, came in and changed very little about the team. Same offense and same defense, same assistant coaches, same players—everything was much the same, except one thing. Collier started to keep and post the score! He and his assistant coaches closely graded every player's performances. Then, on Wednesday mornings when we reported to practice, the score was posted in big letters on a huge board for everyone to see. For defensive linemen we were graded on number of sacks, tackles, assisted tackles, tips (when you deflect the pass), first forces (first one to break through his block and rush the quarterback), and anything else they thought up to grade. All were posted in big letters on the board for all to see. We improved from Paul Brown's firing to a World Championship in 18 months and that was the only difference. When you keep score, the score always improves. In Hebrews 12:1, it says, "Seeing that we are surrounded by such a great crowd of witnesses watching from Heaven, we should run the race well." We averaged 80,000 in home attendance and millions watching on TV, but if you add those in *heaven*, the crowd really gets large. I often thought, with joy, that my Dad had a front-row seat with perfect eye sight and "no pain," able to see his little third-string quarterback become a part of the World Championship team. What we dreamed came true and even more!

In the crisis created by my absence from the Weekend of Champions, when I experienced my close brush with death, the board, the staff, the teammates and every one of our supporters came through. Literally, thousands of people said with one voice that this ministry must continue and grow after I am only a spectator watching from Heaven. This ministry has been, and must continue to be, a powerful work for God. Not to continue my name, or my ministry, but because it is a worthy work, which must thrive until Christ comes again.

Right now, the board is performing at its highest level ever. The staff has never been so strong and the teammates are loyal and backing the ministry to the fullest. The future is brighter than ever! I am growing stronger daily and plan to be fully serving Christ through Champions for Life until I die.

It is pivotal to build strong local teams, which have the responsibility of raising the money and gathering the teammates necessary to reach the prisons and schools in their area. It isn't easy to build a strong local team, but once it is done, they continue to function and accomplish even more than paid staff. Today, we have strong local teams in a number of cities, including Dallas, Fresno, Cleveland, Findlay, Corpus Christi, Austin, and Beaumont, and many others are being developed.

At first, JT Williams and Pete Redmon were pivotal in helping organize our procedure for the future of our growing organization. They will be perhaps even more important to the continuation of the organization long after I'm with the Lord. For several years, JT has served as an unpaid, but fully functional, CFO for Champions for Life. He helped us cut expenses and build our donor base. He spends only a few days per month in our Dallas office, but through the marvels of the computer he is constantly on top of our financial position and watches every penny. In the midst of the recent economic problems, with declining gifts, we have improved our cash position for the last three years. We are becoming stronger financially in spite of it all!

It has become my personal goal, and the goal of the ministry overall, to lift Champions for Life out of debt and put it into a strong position for the future. Our mission is to see the ministry grow so strong that my home-going will only be a boost to the work. The worst thing that could happen is to see the ministry die when the founder dies. Nothing validates the blessing of God like the ministry flourishing when the founder dies. Bill Bright went to Heaven and Campus Crusade is stronger than ever. So shall it be with Champions for Life.

Our board chairman Wayne Stevenson and previous board chairman, Henree Martin say, "With the full backing of the board, we must get totally out of debt before Bill goes to Heaven. We came close to seeing his home-going in February of 2010."

Few inmates ever get a visit from people from the free world, but on a Weekend of Champions they have a lot of time to talk with free-world people. The inmates love it, but the teammates insist that they were the ones most blessed. "I get more out of it than I give," they say.

You may not realize it, but 95 percent of church members never witness to their faith, nor do they lead someone to a rebirth experience with Jesus. But when you give a sincere Christian a good fishing hole and a simple plan of salvation to share, then they can win at the witness game. Obviously, it is not just a game: It is "playing for keeps" for eternity!

If you can show me a way that I can have all my sins forgiven and earn myself a lock on Heaven and no fear of Hell, then I'd be stupid not to aggressively seek it out. But the lost person doesn't see how deadly serious this game is.

So, the Christian, through well-chosen passages from the Bible, can lead the lost person to see his need for salvation. They must be led to the place of the thief who died on the day Jesus did—on the cross, next to Him. He saw His need; he cried out for Jesus to remember him. He was repenting (turning from trust in himself to trust in Christ). He was actually fulfilling everything necessary to "seek first the kingdom" and let everything else be added (Matt 6:33).

In our Weekend of Champions events, we are able to make close contact with people in crisis. Everyone in prison is in crisis. Very few adults make any kind of life-changing decision until they are in crisis. So, prison is the perfect fishing hole. When Christians see the response they are usually "turned on" to finally be witnessing for Christ. Again, they get more out of it than the inmate.

BLESSING FROM THE HEART

From the very beginning of our prison ministry, I noticed a huge hole in the hearts of a surprising number of inmates. They almost always had a father problem. He had deserted them at an early age; he was never there for them, he abused them. Obviously, he inverted the blessing. These fathers actually reversed the blessing and cursed their kids. The inmate could never seem to get over his damaged self-image.

I had a strong, blessing father and mother. I was always around adults who gave me a strong blessing. When my father's death took part of that blessing away, I found myself desperate for a substitute father. They seemed to seek me out. I'm sure this was arranged by the Lord; first my uncle Weldon, then Coach Stages, then Fred Smith.

Fred was the strongest of the three because he had spent his life as a mentor to business and Christian-ministry leaders. Perhaps Fred was more pivotal simply because he served as my friend, mentor, and father substitute longer than the other two. Uncle Weldon stepped in, the first two years after Dad died, then Coach Stages during my three years of High School. But they were only briefly in my "father slot." Even though they were only interim father substitutes, they did help me get through the early pain of fatherlessness. But Fred Smith served in my late college days and continued to be my substitute dad for 50 years (1957 to 2007).

I am a strong believer in the vital role of father substitutes. I've had three, and they were of ultimate importance to me. We have been working to fill this crying need in most inmates, and challenging them to pass it on to their children. Remember, 80 percent of the children of inmates will follow in their parents' footsteps and go to prison also. So we insist that this can only be corrected if they choose to bless their kids. The generational curse doesn't have to be continued. I shout this message in every prison I visit: "It's up to you to bless your kids and keep them out of prisons!"

In the Ring of Champions, we call father substitutes "mentors," and have found them to be an undeniable life-changer for first-time offenders. I know it helps greatly with inmates of any age. Many adult inmates never grow up emotionally. They are stuck in their development from the time they started using drugs or joined the gang, or both! Their age may be 50, but they really never matured. Emotionally, they are stuck back in the days of youth.

Most inmates fail to properly label their problems. "It was someone else's fault," they will say. But I see that weakness in everyone, even among vocational Christian workers and their families. One of our employees at the ministry had a wife who was a sweet lady, but Pollyannaish. Everything had to be perfect and she was straight-laced and legalistic. She was super-idealistic, and was depressed because her super-perfect world was falling apart. She asked to meet with Mavis because she was the evangelist's wife and a spiritually mature woman (several years older). The poor lady opened her heart to Mavis and shared all her problems.

After listening sympathetically for a long time, Mavis said, "Well, I think to start with, you need to label your problems."

"What should I label them?" she questioned.

Mavis answered in a word, "Shit! Don't try to make it good. It is bad and it stinks. Don't try to rationalize it or put the best face on it. Just call it what it is and ask God to help you deal with it in the best way possible. Romans 8:28: 'And we know, that all things...' (Even this stinky situation) can work together for your good and God's glory."

It takes no faith to believe that good things will "work together" for your good. But God tells us, "AND WE KNOW that all things work together for good to them that love God..." (Romans 8:28)— even the obviously bad things.

Mavis made a real friend of the lady because she helped her face her problems realistically. She allowed God to cause even the bad in her life to "work together" in the mix of her life.

Having nine feet of my colon removed wasn't difficult to label: It was a stinky thing (no pun intended), but in the mix of life it will turn out to my good and God's glory! At times it is a stretch to actually see how things will "work together for good." It has to be done by faith. At the time, I didn't really feel thankful. I had to exercise my faith.

NEW CHALLENGES, NEW BLESSINGS

New challenges have presented themselves in our ministry to prisons following the 9/11 attacks. Jose Padilla, a former Chicago gang member who was accused of plotting to set off a radioactive "dirty" bomb in the United States, converted to Islam while in a Florida jail. Richard Reid, who pleaded guilty to trying to blow up a jetliner with a shoe bomb, converted to an extreme form of Islam while in prison in London. Officials say that they can't afford to ignore the extremism that seems to be brewing in the prison system.

The FBI says terrorists regard United States prisons as an ideal place to find groups hostile to the government. They report that radical propaganda flourishes in these groups. Some 10 to 20 percent of inmates are followers of Islam. When inmates come to Christ, they don't become radicalized, because there is a strong and consistent doctrine in Christianity, loving everyone, and certainly never hurting others. We see a lot of converts to Christ among those who follow Islam as a way of protection, but who aren't strong in their faith. We see very few of the more committed Muslims coming to Christ. We must reach them before they become radicalized.

CHAPTER 8

CFT AND ROC

BOB PATTERSON

The one man who was able to bridge all of our ministries—city-wides, prisons, and schools, and youth at risk—was one of the biggest men I ever met, physically, mentally, and spiritually. Bob Patterson was a giant of a man in every way: Almost seven feet tall and a great college basketball player. He was an excellent, well-balanced Christian. He was successful in his computer business and active in Champions for Life. He was faithful to the Weekend of Champions in spite of his busy life.

He was a natural board member with his athletic background and great wisdom. Ultimately he became board chairman for three years before his untimely death at the age of 49, from cancer. He helped us through a lot of difficult staff changes and a trying time in the ministry. Since his death, his lovely and dedicated wife, Trish, has taken his place on our board.

During Bob's last days I visited him several times in Houston and Knoxville, Tennessee and remember two things that were amazing. Fred Morgan accompanied me and said, "Well, Bill, he taught us tonight how a Christian man should face death." He knew his time was short, but he had no fear. He said, with genuine peace and a smile,

"Well, it is a win-win situation, for to me, to live is Christ, and to die is gain (Phil 1:21)."

The second thing he said was, "Bill, I want you to watch Trish, don't let her marry some jerk." I laughingly agreed, but he repeated that the very last day I saw him.

He had a way of seeing an overall picture and keeping all four areas of the ministry totally balanced. He was obviously excited about school ministry, which we call Champions for Today.

Oh, just for your information, I have been successful in keeping all the jerks away from Trish. She is such a classy lady they probably know it's a waste of their time to try to date her. Even though she is beautiful, and still young, she has already lived and loved with the greatest human I've ever known! No one could come close enough to interest her. This is my warning to any interested jerks (ha)!

CHAMPIONS FOR TODAY

In mid-1993, Mike McCoy received a phone call from me. He expressed interest in partnering with us to begin a youth division as a preventative arm of our ministry. I invited him to a directors meeting where he outlined the proposal. He had been conducting school assembly programs for Sports World Ministries as a platform speaker for eight years, so we followed that same pattern with the new division of the ministry.

With board approval, he joined the staff on October 15, 1993. The new division of the Bill Glass Ministries that conducted school assemblies was named Champions for Today. At most school programs, students voluntarily complete comment cards where they indicate their responses to the program. They tell us of their struggles and how they have been encouraged by what the speaker has shared. At one middle school in the Chicago area, over 50 comments about suicide were received.

Board member Ed Hayden enthusiastically attached himself as the liaison between Champions for Today and Bill Glass Ministries. Originally he had no interest in prison ministries; however, after his first reluctant trip to the platform as a speaker, he was hooked. Mike found the prisons a refreshing change from his school programs.

Another board member of our ministry, Lou Korom, caught the vision of Champions for Today and bravely did advance work in the schools of inner-city Chicago, offering them Champions for Today programs. He has sponsored an average of two events per year since the beginning. In each event, the assemblies are presented in at least three schools per day for three days, so the assemblies are presented in at least nine schools in each event, which reaches an average of 5,000 students per event!

Keith Davis came on staff full time not too long ago. Prior to that, he had been a school speaker as needed. He is an African-American who does a great job in the assemblies with his feats of strength and an interesting message! He admitted, "White, 77-year-old Lou Korom goes into some of the worst ghettos in the inner cities, where even I would fear going!" Lou shrugged, "I'm on God's business. He will take care of me; there is nothing to fear. Besides, there's a certain comfort in having a 235 pound black power lifter along with me." He is also the head coach of the local Chicago area team that runs the Cook County Jail Weekend of Champions annually.

Board member Jack Ridge also sponsored Champions for Today many times in Findlay, Ohio. He served as a key leader in three city-wides in 1970, 1979, and 1989, and is a great friend. He has been a board member for 40 years, along with his wife, Judy, also a board member. They both serve as teammates down in the trenches on the front lines for many Weekends of Champions.

Mike McCoy's involvement with Weekends of Champions and Days of Champions has afforded him the opportunity to meet teammates, many of whom have partnered with CFT to bring the message of hope to schools in their areas. He has enjoyed his role as a platform speaker, recruiting teammates at churches and helping build First Team membership.

RING OF CHAMPIONS

In 2000 Bill Glass Champions for Life started researching the need for a program targeted at young people who were at risk of becoming juvenile offenders. The need was brought to the ministry by a judge in Houston who claimed he was seeing several hundred kids in his court every week. It was decided that there was a great need for a preemptive program; however, no new programs could be started unless there was funding available.

Dick Swantner, Champions for Life board member, started to pray about the program and God touched his heart. He decided he would set out to raise the start-up funding for the program.

Dick, an avid hunter and outdoorsman, was sitting in his living room when the spirit spoke to him. He was seeking God's direction, and as he thought and prayed he realized he was staring unconsciously at his gun cabinet. Swantner had quite a collection of guns, and as he was looking at the cabinet, the spirit of God moved upon him to sell one of his prized shotguns to raise the start-up funds.

Dick had been totally sold out to our overall ministry from the beginning. He was the moving force in the second city-wide we conducted in Corpus Christi. He was always involved in the Weekend of Champions to the hilt. One time in San Antonio, on an especially hot day, he was sitting on an outside basketball court for an extended time and burned his bottom badly! We kidded him about being the only man who "burned his butt for Jesus!" He asked his son, Michael, to be the leader for our assembly programs in Corpus Christi schools. Michael has been the quarterback there for 13 years, in charge of over 115 assemblies for Champions for Today!

With funds in hand the ministry hired Ralph McMullen, a former Texas Department of Criminal Justice chaplain, to oversee the startup. The ministry explored the idea of launching the program in Houston. After visiting with the judge, it became obvious that he was not comfortable with the faith-based approach, but we knew it must be a pivotal part of the solution. After that meeting, Ralph and Dick decided to approach the courts in Corpus Christi, their hometown.

In January of 2001, a judge agreed to send 16 juvenile offenders through our brand new Ring of Champions program. She hoped it might do a better job than the other alternatives available to her. The judge herself monitored the event, which was held in the juvenile justice center gym. She was mightily impressed with the program, which featured Keith Davis performing feats of strength and offering a great message about how to do a U-turn in life. From that day onward, she began sending every eligible young person who appeared before her court through our program. She was particularly impressed with what started as a 12-week mentoring program by the trained mentors. As the young mentors progressed, their mentors stayed with them weekly for six to nine months until graduation from the program.

Bi-monthly, about 300 kids are sent to the Ring of Champions program, which has its first meeting with the kids on a Saturday. They arrive at 9 a.m. in the gym of the Corpus Christi juvenile detention center. The kids and their parents and mentors are then entertained by one member of the platform team from the Weekend of Champions.

While Keith Davis is a favorite, many of our Weekend of Champions platform team members have performed for the Ring of Champions opening program. When I have spoken to this group, I am always thrilled to see kids and their parents getting into the mentoring program, which follows the opener. Many of the parents are reached with the gospel and most all of the offenders come to Christ.

A large percentage of the offenders get a mentor, someone trained extensively by the program director, Ralph McMullen. They meet weekly for 12 weeks, but often the relationships continue for years. The mentor often functions as a substitute parent.

There is usually a band that performs in this first program, as well as a dramatic play enacted on the subjects of gangs, drugs, family, etc… Ex-offenders and former Ring of Champions graduates perform in the plays and they are brutally honest and believable, because the performers are ex-cons or gang-bangers themselves!

The judge's enthusiasm sparked strong interest among other judges. By the end of 2003, several of them were sending all the eligible young people appearing in their courts to the Ring of Champions program.

Today in Corpus Christi, some 300 first-offender youth attend each event. Ring of Champions is having a profound impact on crime in Nueces County. Not only does the program save thousands of tax dollars a year, by reducing recidivism, it directly impacts juvenile crime, as well as restores young people to a productive role in the community.

Today Ring of Champions is operating across Texas and several other states. To date the program has maintained a recidivism rate of under eight percent among the kids who are mentored and complete the program.

**A case file from the Nueces County Ring of Champions
mentoring initiative:**

Meet Ring of Champions Mentee: Enrique Macias

Age: 18

Hometown: Corpus Christi, Texas

Occupation: Cabinet Shop Worker

Family: Lives with his mother and four older siblings. One of nine children.

History: Enrique's first brush with trouble came at age 14, when he was picked up for shoplifting. After a series of run-ins with the law, at 16, he was charged with burglary and incarcerated for nine months in the Nueces County Juvenile Detention Center.

There, he met Ring of Champions Teammate and Mentor Brad Condit. "When I was incarcerated, every Monday, Brad would come visit me. He'd assign me something to read. After I'd finish, we'd talk about the moral behind it. You don't trust anyone when you first start out in Boot Camp. But when someone teaches you the kinds of things Brad taught me, it's kind of hard not to trust them. Brad helped me with the things that were tripping me up. He helped me have strength. [Mentoring] is one of the best relationships you could have. Brad taught me some of the best things I could learn — lessons from the Bible, who God is, and accepting Him.

"I'm working now and trying to help my mom as much as I can. Our relationship is a lot better. Before, she was always worried about me. I just got my GED and I'll be applying to join the Air Force. If I don't get in, I'm going to start college this summer.

"Brad and I still stay in touch. I know now that staying in church is a priority. When I don't go, I get spiritually weak. I took my cousin and I've invited some of my friends. I make it a priority to read my Bible daily. "I don't really know where my life would have led me if I hadn't met Brad. I don't think about that. I just look forward now."

CHAPTER 9

CHRISTIAN TALIBAN

There is a constant challenge facing the Christian athlete on a football team to relate to non-Christians without seeming to apply pressure. If your teammate feels you are judging and censoring his conduct, he can never be open to you.

THE BLESSINGS OF NOT BEING THE TALIBAN

A sports commentator told of meeting Tim Tebow at the NFL combine and how embarrassed he was for cussing in Tim's presence. I had the same problem 40 years ago. But I came to a different way of handling it. I was determined not to become a moral policeman. Beginning my NFL career with Detroit, I was too judgmental of those around me. I decided to try and fit in better when I played for the Cleveland Browns. I became a much better teammate to the players, and even performed better on the field. When I was with the Browns, I was more adaptable because I changed my mindset.

If people stop cussing around me, they are not being themselves. I actually came to resent those who would force me into being a moral policeman, standing in judgment of the way people talk. If all non-

Christians in the world stopped cussing, all you'd have is a bunch of non-cussing pagans. The need is not to stop cussing; it is to trust Christ personally for forgiveness and salvation. The need is not a moral change; the need is new birth in Christ. Anything less is an actual detriment to the cause. The Taliban has moral policemen that enforce their narrow minded code. It is a different version of the Pharisees from New Testament times. Unfortunately, there are those in Christian circles today who are what I would call the Christian Taliban.

If a person could pay five dollars as the price of forgiveness and eternal life, it wouldn't be just or fair, because half the world doesn't even have five dollars to spare! If you had to do good works, then again, which good works and how much? I've even heard those who say, "If my good deeds outweigh my bad deeds in the final judgment, I'll be fine."

Man is constantly trying to devise a way to merit redemption. Above all, he doesn't easily submit to grace (unmerited favor). Everyone thinks they have to earn their salvation (Eph 2:8 and 9). If you had to be intelligent-an I.Q. above 120, that too would be unjust; some are slow mentally. Good looking? Also unjust; some are ugly. (That would cut me out for sure!)

The only thing that is totally fair is "faith." Anyone can believe. Satan wants to keep adding to God's simple plan of salvation, but it is faith and nothing more. I wrote Tim Tebow a letter and said, "Don't let the legalist spoil your effectiveness." I hope he listens. It will help him to fit in better and be a whole lot more influential! Maybe it's none of my business, but I would hope he could learn from my failures at Detroit and my victories in Cleveland.

Most non-Christians have a "works" concept of salvation. Until this is changed they cannot be born again: "They, being ignorant of God's righteousness and going about to establish their own righteousness, do not submit themselves to the righteousness of God" Romans 10:3 (referred to here as "God's righteousness"). The only righteousness that is efficacious (effective toward salvation) is the redemptive work of Christ alone. It is never your own righteousness. Ephesians 2:8-9 says that if you could get good enough then you could brag about it. So you hear people say, "I'm as good as anyone else," or "I'm trying to be a Christian." Works, again!

Tim Tebow is one fantastic athlete, leader, and Christian, influencing millions. I rejoice in his blessings and shudder at what he is facing. I was a lot like Tebow at the same stage of life, only he was more famous for being a quarterback. More famous, more headlines, more pressure, more money, and so his potential for good and bad simply multiplies. Why do I also feel sorry for him? Because along with the glory and blessing comes a great deal of pressure and responsibility. He is handling it so very well, but Satan will fight him every step of the way. Even his slightest misstep will be blown out of proportion.

Everyone will want him to speak to their club, church, football banquet, in schools, and even prisons. He'll have to learn to say "No!" or it will kill him. I spoke almost every night from the December when I was named consensus All-American to June when I graduated from Baylor. They were all great opportunities, but it was too much. I had to be my best on the field to validate my witness. I was representing the Lord by the way I played. If I wasn't my very best as a football player, it actually hurt the cause.

BATTLING WORKS

All pagans, and most Christians, have a tendency to fall victim to some type of moral attainment. Christians have a continuous job of retraining others to get away from this false idea of conversion. Non-Christians usually think of Christians as moral policemen. I've learned that the Pharisee is never a good influence, because he is constantly reinforcing "works" theology and heaping guilt on the non-Christian, and thus creating resentment.

It's not how righteous you are; it's a matter of knowing and understanding and experiencing God's grace. I would say, "Look, if you normally cuss, then please, cuss around me. I can't forgive you; only God can. If you stop cussing, but don't come to know Christ, you are still lost. Again, as simply a non-cussing, lost person, you're no better off, or maybe even worse, you are really further away from God. Romans 10:3 states, "Still going about to establish your own righteousness, still ignorant of God's righteousness."

A RADICAL WITNESS

When I was playing in the NFL, a teammate asked me, "Bill, I have this beautiful neighbor whose husband travels a lot. She is trying to seduce me; what should I do?"

Deciding to take a radical approach, I answered: "I think you should say yes."

He yelled out loud to everyone on our charter flight, which was full of players, coaches and sportswriters: "Bill says I should sleep with my neighbor's wife!"

Then I came to my true point. "Let me tell you why," I said. "If you don't, then you'll be self-righteous, and Pharisees are the hardest to reach. But if you do cheat on your wife, it will probably make your life fall apart. Your wife and kids and even grandkids will hate you. Then maybe you'll hit rock bottom and you'll look up to God."

I explained that I certainly could not commit adultery because as a Christian I'm answerable to God and he would say it's a sin and violation of His commandment.

In the past, this has caused me some unexpected consternation. For example, at my eldest son's 50th birthday. His wife, Laura planned a big birthday party for Billy. She invited more people than their house could accommodate and several people came invited by friends. Anyway, the house was jammed with people, a few sitting, and most standing so we were squeezed in shoulder to shoulder. I was shoulder to shoulder with a beautiful young lady whose husband had died three years earlier. I had done some counseling with her son who was a huge, young athlete. He was taller than me, at least 6'8". He was my grandson Josh's friend.

I opened the conversation with a series of sincere compliments about her outstanding son. Naturally, she loved that. Then, I launched into trying to help her with her grief. She quickly admitted her pain and hurt. I was seeking to be a good listener. I was glad I had at least some counseling training at seminary. First, seek to empathize. Second, refer to those better trained, and third, make certain to realize that if you are helpful, a female may be so appreciative of your help that she could transfer that appreciation into romantic feelings. Above all, the good pastoral counselor should never be flattered by this reaction. Be sure to never counsel privately with the opposite sex.

As we spoke, I was gratified to think how valuable my training in pastoral counseling had been over the years. To my amazement this lovely young widow was touching my butt. Since we were forced to stand shoulder to shoulder I thought at first it was just an accident. But then she began to grab one entire cheek, firmly! I became increasingly embarrassed, realizing this was no accidental contact. I could feel my face flushing and turning red. I was really sweating. Then I looked down to see for sure that she was massaging my rear end. I started to ask her to quit. I rehearsed what I would say in my head, "Dear, I know you are at a most stressful time of your life, but I must ask you to not touch me in that way!" Just then, I looked closer to see my teenaged grandson had crawled beneath the crowd and was the culprit! I was so relieved that I had to tell everyone in the group that my grandson, Caleb, had totally fooled me, and everyone had a huge laugh at my expense, especially him (who like most of my grandkids loved to tease me).

The joke was good, but the issue's a serious one. Adultery is forbidden by the seventh commandment. There is nothing in the New Testament to weaken this commandment. Christ himself even made it stronger by saying that even the thought of adultery is sin. I told my teammate, "I fear God and my wife, and I really don't know who I fear the most. But you aren't a Christian, so you are making up your own rules as you go along. All your human efforts at righteousness simply add to your lostness. Being a Christian isn't 'not sleeping with your neighbor,' being a Christian is knowing Christ personally. Once you become a Christian, this commandment will apply to you, but now it doesn't. So until you hit bottom, you probably won't look up to God. If you cheat you'll make a junkyard of your later years and you'll hit bottom and that will be when you'll look up to God! So the quicker you hit bottom and the harder you fall the better, because then you'll look up to God."

THE REST OF THE STORY

We had only seen each other once since we left the NFL. It was at a dinner in New York. He said, "Do you remember suggesting to me that I should cheat on my wife?"

I replied, "Sure I do. But do you remember why?"

He said, "Clearly. You said Christianity is knowing Christ, not living a good life by keeping the commandments.

"But the other thing I shall never forget is that you predicted if I cheated, my life would probably fall apart, and it has. I just divorced my third wife, I'm broke, and have no job, all my wives, kids, and grandkids hate me. My life has fallen apart."

I shrugged and said, "Well, you have obviously hit bottom, so it is time to look up to God." He agreed. The shock approach caused him to remember, but I believe it is totally scriptural.

If I had tried to point out the foolishness of cheating sexually, he would have laughed in my face and done it anyway. But he did remember, even after 20 years, my pointing out the difference between morality and Christianity. Now I certainly believe that knowing Christ ought to change the way we live. I repeat, if the non-Christian simply copies Christian morality, he is no better off. In fact, he really may be worse off, because he has a false, "works-based" theology. He thinks that trying to do right to get right with God is the way to go.

CHOOSE TO BE THE COUNSELOR, NOT THE ASSISTANT PRINCIPAL

I've noticed that in high schools the assistant principal and the counselor are always two different people. Why? The assistant principal always handles the discipline and the counselor is the one you admit your problems to. You aren't going to open up and admit your problems to someone whose role is to discipline you. You can never censor people's conduct and be a good witness at the same time.

Mother Teresa is beloved, and the Taliban with their moral police force is hated. Everybody loves Jesus and hates the Pharisees. Christ seemed to lean toward all the ones that the Pharisees looked down on. The only one with a right to look down on others was Christ, for He alone was without sin. Yes, He had the right, but He never did! He never looked down or spoke down to anyone. He always ended up siding with sinners. The woman at the well, according to the Pharisees, was a slut with five husbands, but Christ saw her as an evangelist and she brought many people in that town to Christ (John 4).

Cleaning up the morality of our world is a hopeless cause. The Bible teaches that morals will only grow worse until Christ comes again. I used to think when I first became a Christian that it was my job to clean up all evil. Now, I know that it is one of Satan's ways of diverting me from my main purpose. If we try to force Christian morality on a pagan world, it will only make them hate us and promote the false theology of works.

When I first went to the Browns, I had a friend who didn't drink, smoke, cheat on his wife, or even cuss. I thought he'd make a great Christian. There would be very little moral change necessary for him to become Christian. But, as far as I know, he never trusted Christ. There was another teammate, the biggest hell-raiser on the team, whom I thought was beyond hope. But he, in recent years, has trusted Christ and is now a leader in his church. It is a total mistake to think that it should be easy to win the morally straight people to the Lord, on the premise that would have to change only slightly to follow Christ. These people are usually trusting in their own goodness, and that is always counterproductive. Maybe the hell-raiser is searching for something in all the wrong places. As unattractive as the Taliban is, sending out its police force to enforce their morality, there are Christians who are much like the Taliban. In fact, I call them the Christian Taliban. If a person cusses, drinks, smokes, doesn't go to church enough, fails to give to the right cause, he is censored by the Christian Taliban. Where does that leave him?

MY SECOND MEETING WITH GOVERNOR CLEMENTS

In 1964, I was invited to speak at a football banquet in Nashville, Tennessee. The lieutenant governor attended the banquet and asked me to come over to the capital and speak to the State Senate the next morning. When I got through with my speech, I was handed a note from Governor Clements, asking me to have coffee with him in his office in the capital.

He warmly greeted me and leaned back in his huge leather office chair with his legs crossed at the ankles, smoking an overly long cigar. He opened the conversation by expressing how much he appreciated my thoughtful trip to the Tennessee dressing room. He reminded me of the 1957 Sugar Bowl game when we beat the No. 2 team in the nation, Tennessee. Fortunately, the player that was kicked wasn't hurt badly, but it did look nasty at the time. I changed the subject by saying, "I understand you are close friends with Billy Graham."

He launched into a long and fascinating story about how Graham had played golf with him recently at a local country club, and at noon he suggested they go downtown for lunch.

"Why can't we just have lunch here?" Billy asked.

"The only place is in the bar," the Governor explained.

Billy teased, "I'm not thinking of a drink for lunch. I just want a sandwich." So they went into the bar for lunch. During that meal, Billy asked to switch seats with the governor. He asked why Billy wanted to switch seats. Graham explained, "I think that guy at the bar would enjoy his drink more looking at a politician rather than a preacher." When the governor asked for more explanation, Graham said he really didn't want to make people feel guilty. He didn't want to play God and tell people what to eat and drink. Colossians 2:16 says, "Let no men judge you according to what you may eat or drink."

The governor went on to say, "Billy called me recently because he knew I was an authority on Sam Houston. He asked me to send him all I could about the connection to his mother's grandfather, Reverend Baines. I sent him six pages of material, which he used years later at President Johnson's prayer breakfast during his inauguration."

Evidently, while Sam Houston was governor of Tennessee, he decided to get right with God. He called two Presbyterian pastors in to talk to him. He earnestly asked their guidance as to how to find salvation. They said they understood he was considering a divorce. They would rather know why before they went further with their discussion. Houston leaned forward, drawing the ministers in close to him and asking in a low tone, "Can you keep a secret?" They assured him they could. He said, "So can I!" he picked them up and threw them bodily out of the room. He was a big man with a big temper.

Sam Houston never considered spiritual matters again until the last 15 years of his life. He had served as governor of Texas, the only man to be governor of two states (Tennessee and Texas). He even served as a United States Senator from Texas. But, late in life, he went to hear Pastor Baines in his little Baptist church in Independence, Texas. As a result of hearing the gospel, he trusted Christ and wrote a letter of appreciation to Pastor Baines. There is today a yellowing framed letter, on a White House wall in the Oval Office, from Sam Houston to Pastor Baines thanking him for leading him to the Lord. President Lyndon Baines Johnson was named after his mother's grandfather, Reverend George Washington Baines, who led Sam Houston to faith in Christ.

There is also a pew marked "Sam Houston's Pew" in the First Baptist Church of Independence, Texas. His name was crudely carved by Houston with his Bowie knife well over 100 years ago.

EPILOGUE

Earlier in this book I described myself as a big, beached whale, so deathly ill I was only able to open one eye. Those circumstances left me to wonder how the sickness and surgery that put me on the shelf for a while could possibly "work together" (Romans 8:28).

God has already shown me several ways. First, to find ways to serve God and others. Prior to this, I had not slowed down enough for many things in my hurried life to be recognized. Already I've realized several things, like the value of writing this book, spending more time with the family, spending more time in prayer and study, and spending time with God, and maybe ways I hadn't even had time to think of or God to lead me to.

DRESS REHEARSAL

It was like a "dress rehearsal." Everyone stepped forward and functioned like real champions. I wrote a note to the board and staff in which I pointed this out.

"I've noticed that since I came near death you guys have been rising to the challenge," I wrote. "Any way you measure success— number of decisions, number of teammates, and number of inmates reached— we have had real victory. A major donor asked me, 'What happens to the ministry when you go to Heaven?' I've never been surer that we will just pick up speed and grow! Why? Great teammates, great staff, great board of directors, and a great God!"

We always have good success in the ministry of Champions for Life on all our events. God always blesses. But we always seem to drag a little financially, so I'm anxious to get ahead in this area also!

This autobiography covers 75 years. I am amazed as to how often in those years I would discover that God's way is the best way—whether it is cases like that of my NFL teammate cheating on his wife, or other instances throughout my life when "the rest of the story" makes its way back to me. God's way is always best. I've lived long enough to see how things turn out.

Think what Heaven will reveal! In this life we "see through a glass darkly." In Heaven we shall see from God's viewpoint. It will be like watching a parade from the top of a skyscraper. You see the first and last of the parade at the same time. From street level, you see only one or two floats at a time.

When you see the end from the beginning, then you can act with the end in mind. If you know that you'll make a "junkyard of your old age," then you'll be less anxious to cheat. If your wife and kids and even grandchildren hate you because you are a cheater, then maybe knowing what the results will be, you may choose to make "the rest of the story," end differently. Since you always "reap what you sow" then all you must do is change the sowing.

But most people must learn the hard way, through the school of hard knocks. Or better still, from watching others try and fail, as they keep insisting on doing it their way instead of God's. The Bible reveals that all of life is made up of sowing and reaping. If we sow to the wind, we reap the whirlwind. God warned us in His word what will happen. I was able to predict the outcome of my teammate's adultery because it is the dependable law of sowing and reaping as explained in the Bible: "Be sure, your sins will find you out. Whatever a man sows he must reap!"

As I said before, Jesus told a story in Luke 16 about two men who died. If I were telling the story, that would end my story: they died; the End! But Jesus followed them after death into Heaven and Hell. Sure enough, Hell is painfully awful and Heaven is great. The rich man wants to warn his brothers about the seriousness of this life and eternity, to avoid Hell and seek Heaven. But Christ says that if they won't listen to the "prophets of God, then they won't be persuaded by someone risen from the dead to warn them." If Christ rose from the dead, He was God. If He was God, He was certainly truthful about these three things:

1. He is the only way of eternal life.

2. I'm a sinner and I need forgiveness.

3. There is a Heaven for believers and a Hell for unbelievers. By definition, God cannot lie!

Since Jesus places emphasis on this life and the life to come, so should we. Since He believed there was a great audience watching from Heaven (Hebrews 11-12:1) that is cheering us on, I believe we need to get right with God to please Him and that great crowd watching from Heaven's grandstand.

I've always been anxious to use time in the best way possible. I don't know of a way I can find to spend my time better than a Weekend of Champions, and the other phases of our ministry, teaching people to share their faith. Since one soul is worth the whole world, God expects you to be involved in soul salvation. It is obvious that you must be searching for ways of investing your time in evangelism and Christian growth.

Slow down and enjoy the journey. I had to just about die in order to slow down enough to count all of my blessings. Looking back long enough to see God's hand at work is a way to build faith. Since faith is that which pleases God most, it is important to let it be built up by counting and even recounting your blessings. By faith you came to know God in the first place through rebirth (Eph 2:8-9). By faith you walk in Him (Col 2:6). By faith your prayers are answered.

YOU HAVE BEEN MY BLESSING, TOO

Thanks for joining me on this faith-building journey through my 75 years, a journey dedicated to recounting my blessings.

One person I must not leave out is my favorite warden. As I finish the book and this epilogue I cannot forget her.

The best warden I've known through the years is Lucile Plane. She was, for years, the warden at the Mountain View Unit in Gatesville. This was the first women's prison in Gatesville, site of the female psychiatric unit and death row beginning in 1981. Lucile knew every inmate by first and last name, and loved them all. She knew exactly what their crime was and talked to them about it. She'd introduce me to an inmate and give a brief description, for example: "This is Sally, she's a pimp back in Dallas, but she has become a Christian and she's going to quit pimping, aren't you Sally?"

"Yes, Warden, I sure am," the inmate would reply.

Warden Plane has been retired for more than 20 years. I always call her when I go to her unit. They even renamed it Warden Lucile Plane State Jail. It is a large women's prison in East Texas. She now lives in a retirement village in Gatesville, and her friends take care of her well. I go visit her every time we conduct a Weekend of Champions in Gatesville. She is 96 and is doing great. She is like a mother to me. I love her. She, too, has been a blessing.

PHOTO GALLERY

▲Sports page cartoon

▲1956 All Americans – Bill #55, Jim Parker (#62) next to
Bill. Back row – Johnny Majors, John Brodie, Jim Brown

◀Bill Glass Rushing
Bart Starr, Green Bay
Quarterback

Bill Glass Rushing
Steeler's Quarterback
Ed Brown ▶

◀ Sacking Y. A.
Tittle in 1966

Head Coach Blanton
Collier – Always
Teaching ▶

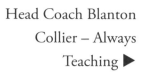

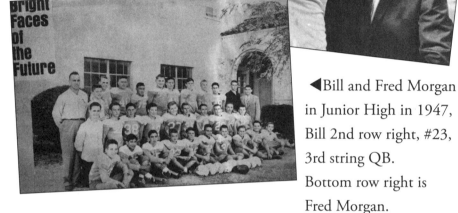

◀Bill and Fred Morgan
in Junior High in 1947,
Bill 2nd row right, #23,
3rd string QB.
Bottom row right is
Fred Morgan.

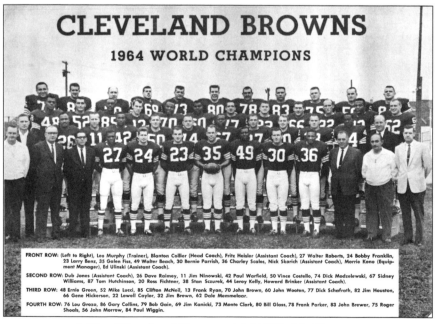

CLEVELAND BROWNS
1964 WORLD CHAMPIONS

FRONT ROW: (Left to Right), Leo Murphy (Trainer), Blanton Collier (Head Coach), Fritz Heisler (Assistant Coach), 27 Walter Roberts, 24 Bobby Franklin, 23 Larry Benz, 35 Galen Fiss, 49 Walter Beach, 30 Bernie Parrish, 36 Charley Scales, Nick Skorich (Assistant Coach), Morrie Kono (Equipment Manager), Ed Ulinski (Assistant Coach).

SECOND ROW: Dub Jones (Assistant Coach), 26 Dave Raimey, 11 Jim Ninowski, 42 Paul Warfield, 50 Vince Costello, 74 Dick Modzelewski, 67 Sidney Williams, 87 Tom Hutchinson, 20 Ross Fichtner, 38 Stan Sczurek, 44 Leroy Kelly, Howard Brinker (Assistant Coach).

THIRD ROW: 48 Ernie Green, 52 Mike Lucci, 85 Clifton McNeil, 13 Frank Ryan, 70 John Brown, 60 John Wooten, 77 Dick Schafrath, 82 Jim Houston, 66 Gene Hickerson, 22 Lowell Caylor, 32 Jim Brown, 62 Dale Memmelaar.

FOURTH ROW: 76 Lou Groza, 86 Gary Collins, 79 Bob Gain, 69 Jim Kanicki, 73 Monte Clark, 80 Bill Glass, 78 Frank Parker, 83 John Brewer, 75 Roger Shoals, 56 John Morrow, 84 Paul Wiggin.

▲The Cleveland Browns 1964 World Champions

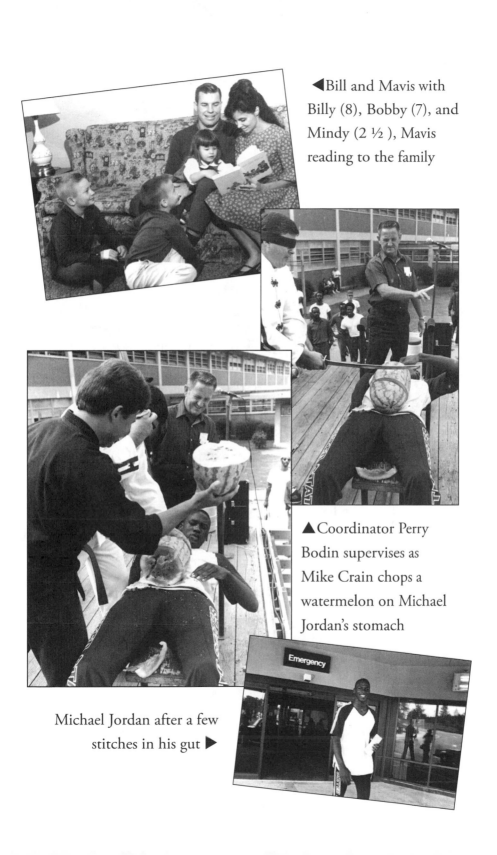

◀Bill and Mavis with Billy (8), Bobby (7), and Mindy (2 ½), Mavis reading to the family

▲Coordinator Perry Bodin supervises as Mike Crain chops a watermelon on Michael Jordan's stomach

Michael Jordan after a few stitches in his gut ▶

Bill Glass speaking
during a City Wide
crusade ▶

◀Rosie Greer at a
military Weekend of
Champions

Bill Glass and
Tom Landry walk
through prison halls
with the wardens ▶

◀Tom Landry shakes an
inmate's hand on death row

◀Steeler's star player
"Mean Joe" Green
serving in prison
on a Weekend of
Champions

Roger Staubach of
the Dallas Cowboys
on a Weekend of
Champions ▶

◀Tanya Crevier
– World's Best
Female Basketball
Handler perform-
ing at prison

Tanya hugging Jack
Eckerd, an early backer of
Champions for Life ▶

Tino Wallenda performing at prison ▶

◀Devin Wyman speaking on the yard to inmates

Mike Singletary speaks to a group of inmates ▶

◀Pencil drawing by Pete Redmond's granddaughter of Bill (front), Pete (back left) and J.T. Williams (back right)

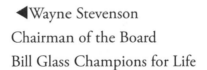

◀Ring of
Champions
Mentor-Mentee

Jack Murphy speaking
at prison in a Weekend
of Champions ▶

◀Wayne Stevenson
Chairman of the Board
Bill Glass Champions for Life

▲Matt-Billy Ray-Josh-(Billy's children)

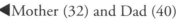
◀Mother (32) and Dad (40)

▲Bill kissing fourth generation (Katy) Mavis,
while second generation Mavis watches proudly.

◀Board Leader, Lou
Korom with his wife
Bonnie, Bill, and CFL
banquet speaker, Tom
Landry

Fred Smith, my
mentor and loved
father substitute ▶

◀Jack Ridge, Board
leader for 40 years,
talking with inmates.

This is the 2011 Bill Glass Champions for Life Executive Management Team.

Pictured from left to right: Jim Marvine (Director of Prison Ministry), Jim Subers (CEO) and Kit Van Arsdale (Director IT and Internal Prison Department Operations). Not Pictured: Ralph McMullen (Director Ring of Champions).

These leaders combine a passion for Christ with considerable skill, and this gives me great confidence in the future of the ministry. Throughout our rich history, God has brought us many dynamic leaders to serve with us in our calling to evangelism. I am grateful to everyone who answered the call to join hands with me to help reach the "least of these" with the Gospel. The future continues to be bright for our ministry, and the need has never been greater.

To join us on one of our exciting events and to learn more, please contact us at:
Bill Glass Champions for Life
P O Box 761101 • Dallas, TX 75376
Phone 972-298-1101
Website: www.billglass.org • Bill's email: billg@billglass.org

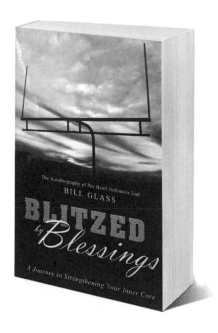

How can you use this book?

MOTIVATE

EDUCATE

THANK

INSPIRE

PROMOTE

CONNECT

Why have a custom version of *Blitzed by Blessings*?

- Build personal bonds with customers, prospects, employees, donors, and key constituencies
- Develop a long-lasting reminder of your event, milestone, or celebration
- Provide a keepsake that inspires change in behavior and change in lives
- Deliver the ultimate "thank you" gift that remains on coffee tables and bookshelves
- Generate the "wow" factor

Books are thoughtful gifts that provide a genuine sentiment that other promotional items cannot express. They promote employee discussions and interaction, reinforce an event's meaning or location, and they make a lasting impression. Use your book to say "Thank You" and show people that you care